DOCTOR · WHO

CREATURES AND DEMONS

BY JUSTIN RICHARDS

BBC
BOOKS

Published in 2007 by BBC Books, an imprint of Ebury Publishing.

Ebury Publishing is a division of the Random House Group.

10 9 8 7 6 5 4 3 2 1

ISBN 9781 84607 229 1

Commissioning Editor:	Mathew Clayton	Design:	Lee Binding
Range Consultant:	Justin Richards	Project Editor:	Vicki McKay
Cover Design:	Lee Binding	Production Manager:	Kenneth McKay

Doctor Who is a BBC Wales production for BBC ONE. Executive Producers: Russell T Davies and Julie Gardner. Producer: Phil Collinson.

Printed and bound in Great Britain by CPI Bath. Colour separations by Dot Gradations, Wickford, England.

BBC Books would like to thank the following for providing photographs and for permission to reproduce copyright material. While every effort has been made to trace and acknowledge all copyright holders, we would like to apologise should there have been any errors or omissions.

All images copyright © BBC, except:

pages 37 and 39 Miss Susan Moore

page 67 (top) Charles Lumm

pages 78 and 82 (main) Mat Irvine

All production designs and storyboards are reproduced courtesy of the Doctor Who Art Department. Images on pages 9 (both top), 20 (bottom), 36, 44, 45, 46 and 65 are courtesy of Millennium FX.

All computer-generated imagery courtesy of The Mill, including the images on pages 12, 17 (top), 18 (bottom), 20 (top), 21 (top, middle right, bottom), 25 (bottom left), 33 (top), 47 (top, middle), 51 (top), 54 (left middle), 55, 64 (top), 71 (top), 73 (left), 74 and 75.

With additional thanks to:

Will Cohen, Russell T Davies, Cameron Fitch, Neill Gorton, Ian Grutchfield, Clayton Hickman and all at *Doctor Who Magazine*, David J. Howe, Peter McKinstry, Isobel McLean, Marianne Paton, Helen Raynor, Edward Russell, Gary Russell, Matthew Savage, Edward Thomas, Mike Tucker

And in loving memory of Craig Hinton

CONTENTS

'I am the sin, and the temptation, and the desire. I am the pain and the loss and the death of hope. I have been imprisoned for eternity, but no more. The Pit is open. And I am free.'

The Beast in *The Impossible Planet*

This is the third volume to explore the monstrous enemies and ghastly alien villains that the Doctor has faced in his journeys throughout time and space. As in *Monsters and Villains* and *Aliens and Enemies*, you will find background data on the creatures, details of what happened when the Doctor encountered them, and behind-the-scenes information on all eras of **Doctor Who** – from the Celestial Toymaker, who threatened the very first Doctor in the 1960s, through to the Doctor's most recent run-in with his arch enemies, the Daleks, in Manhattan in 1930.

As well as his newest adversaries, such as the Carrionites and the Judoon, you can learn about the terrifying Destroyer – Lord of Darkness and the Eater of Worlds – as well as the Beast, imprisoned in the Satan Pit for eternity, since before the dawn of time.

You can discover how the Macra have changed since the Doctor first met them – both within the narrative of the stories *The Macra Terror* and *Gridlock*, and in terms of how the terrifying creatures were brought to life for television.

And as you share his adventures and relive the excitement, you can see how the Doctor, too, has changed and moved on – from one incarnation to the next regeneration, from his unstated, unstatable love for Rose Tyler to his growing friendship and deep respect for Martha Jones.

Come with us and see the most extraordinary sights – and the most amazing creatures – of the universe. Or, as the Doctor himself supposedly once said: 'Stay behind – and regret your staying until the day you die …'

THE ABZORBALOFF

The Abzorbaloff comes from Clom, the twin planet of Raxacoricofallapatorius. A hideous, green humanoid creature it can absorb other life forms just by touching them. Once absorbed, the Abzorbaloff has access to their knowledge and experience. It is desperate to find and absorb the Doctor, believing he will be the ultimate 'meal' and provide him with a wealth of experience.

For a while the victims of the Abzorbaloff are still visible – as faces embedded in its skin. They retain some individuality, and can talk and even read the Abzorbaloff's thoughts. Ultimately, the Abzorbaloff is destroyed by the combined will of its victims working together to pull it apart.

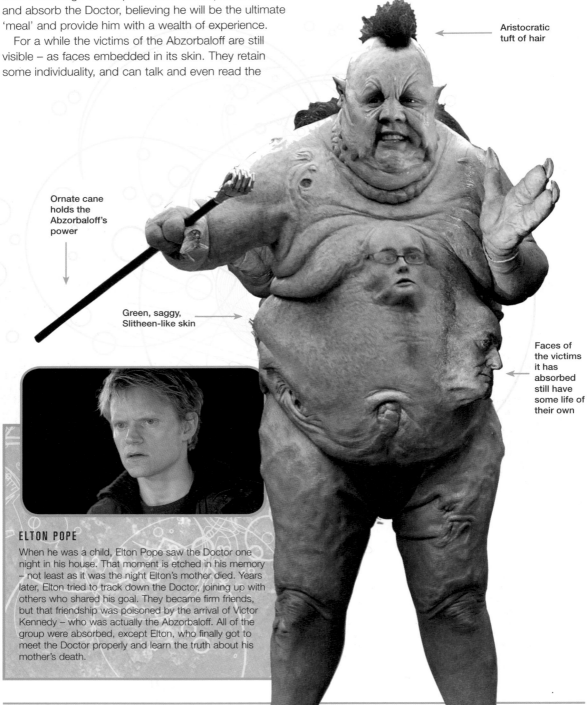

Aristocratic tuft of hair

Ornate cane holds the Abzorbaloff's power

Green, saggy, Slitheen-like skin

Faces of the victims it has absorbed still have some life of their own

ELTON POPE

When he was a child, Elton Pope saw the Doctor one night in his house. That moment is etched in his memory – not least as it was the night Elton's mother died. Years later, Elton tried to track down the Doctor, joining up with others who shared his goal. They became firm friends, but that friendship was poisoned by the arrival of Victor Kennedy – who was actually the Abzorbaloff. All of the group were absorbed, except Elton, who finally got to meet the Doctor properly and learn the truth about his mother's death.

LOVE & MONSTERS

Elton Pope meets up with several other people who are trying to find the Doctor, and together they form a group called LINDA. Gradually, they come to spend less time looking for the Doctor and more having fun. Then the mysterious Victor Kennedy arrives and sets himself up as their leader, organising them to renew their search. Elton tracks down Rose's mother, Jackie, but she realises what he is up to and warns Rose.

By the time the Doctor and Rose find Elton, Victor Kennedy has revealed himself to be the Abzorbaloff, and has absorbed all the other members of the group. But together, their faces embedded in the creature's skin, they are able to tear it apart.

Written by
Russell T Davies
Featuring
Elton Pope, with the
Tenth Doctor and Rose
First broadcast
17 June 2006
1 episode

LINDA

Elton makes up the name LINDA, which stands for London Investigation 'N' Detective Agency. Its members – Mr Skinner, Ursula, Bliss, Bridget and Elton – are trying to discover everything they can about the Doctor, but as they become friends they get distracted. Mr Skinner reads extracts from his novel, Bliss shows off her sculpture, Bridget supplies home-cooked food. They even form a band and perform old ELO hits.

But the arrival of Victor Kennedy refocuses them on finding the Doctor – with disastrous consequences.

THE HOIX

When Elton finds the Doctor and Rose, having heard reports of a police box turning up in Woolwich, they are battling against the alien Hoix. Little is known about the Hoix, although it is partial to pork chops. Elton witnesses the Doctor and Rose trying to calm the Hoix by throwing liquid from a red bucket over it.

The Doctor pauses in his task when he sees – and recognises – Elton. Scared, Elton runs off. Moments later he hears the TARDIS dematerialise – the Hoix, presumably, has been dealt with.

THE HOWLING HALLS

When the Doctor rescues Elton from the Abzorbaloff, it is the second time he saves Elton's life. The first was when Elton was a child, the night he saw the Doctor in his house – the night his mother died. There was a living shadow in the Popes' house, an elemental shade that had escaped from the Howling Halls. The Doctor stopped it, but was too late to save Elton's mother.

Since that first glimpse of the Doctor, Elton Pope has yearned to discover more about the mysterious wanderer in time and space.

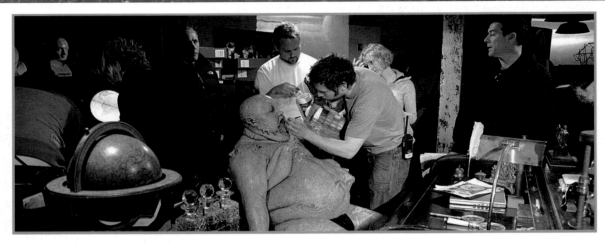

CREATING THE ABZORBALOFF

Neill Gorton's Millennium FX team created both the Abzorbaloff and the hideous Hoix. As with almost all the alien creatures to appear in **Doctor Who**, the Hoix was created to fulfil its role and description in the script. Put together largely from bits and pieces 'left over' from other monsters, it was, nonetheless, an impressive creation by the Millennium FX team.

The Abzorbaloff, however, was devised very differently: it did not spring from the mind of the writer and the pages of the script. It was, in fact, devised by young William Grantham as his entry in a competition to design a **Doctor Who** monster, run by the popular children's BBC television programme **Blue Peter**. The prize was for William to see his creation appear in an episode of **Doctor Who**.

Top: The Abzorbaloff gets some final make-up treatment.
Above: William Grantham's winning design.
Right: The Abzorbaloff on location.

Left: Completed model of the Abzorbaloff.
Below: A full sculpture is made.
Bottom: Designs for Kennedy's cane.

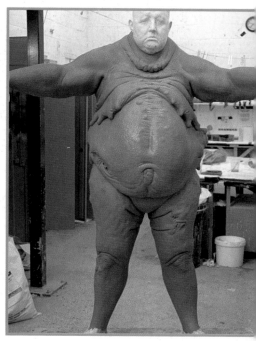

SCRIPT EXTRACT

It's still Victor's face, just about, but in the body of a vile, green creature; THE ABZORBALOFF. It has wailing, lost faces embedded in its skin.

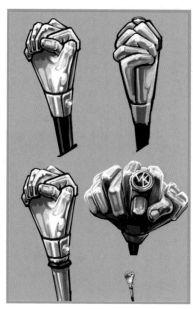

The design that William submitted was turned into a costume by Millennium FX, and sculpted to fit comedian and actor Peter Kay, who played both Kennedy and the Abzorbaloff itself. The faces of the creature's victims were sculpted into the costume – complete with mouths that could move. For close-up shots, Simon Greenall (Mr Skinner) and Shirley Henderson (Ursula Blake) pushed their faces into a specially built prop of a piece of the Abzorbaloff's body. A similar method was used to achieve the effect of Ursula's face embedded in a paving stone.

Russell T Davies set himself several challenges when writing *Love & Monsters*. Not only did it have to include the winning **Blue Peter** entry – and, of course, no one knew what that would be until the winner was chosen – but the story would also feature very little of the Doctor or Rose. This was because the filming of the 2006 series of **Doctor Who** was scheduled so that *Love & Monsters* was shot while other episodes were also being made (*The Impossible Planet* and *The Satan Pit* – see page 50), so the lead actors would have little time to spare.

The result was a very unusual **Doctor Who** story indeed, with Elton Pope – played by Marc Warren – taking centre stage in his struggle to find the Doctor and escape the Abzorbaloff.

THE ALIEN AMBASSADORS

The Alien Ambassadors are sent to Earth in the place of human astronauts returning from a mission to Mars – but they, in turn, are kidnapped from the landed space capsule. (It seems as though the 'astronauts' have been infected with a deadly form of radiation, because when they reappear they can kill people merely by touching them.)

The Ambassadors were kidnapped by forces opposed to contact between Earth and the aliens, and are being forced to kill, to make it seem as if they are hostile. But on board their mothership, where the real astronauts are being held, the aliens believe that mankind has imprisoned their ambassadors. If they are not returned, the aliens will destroy Earth.

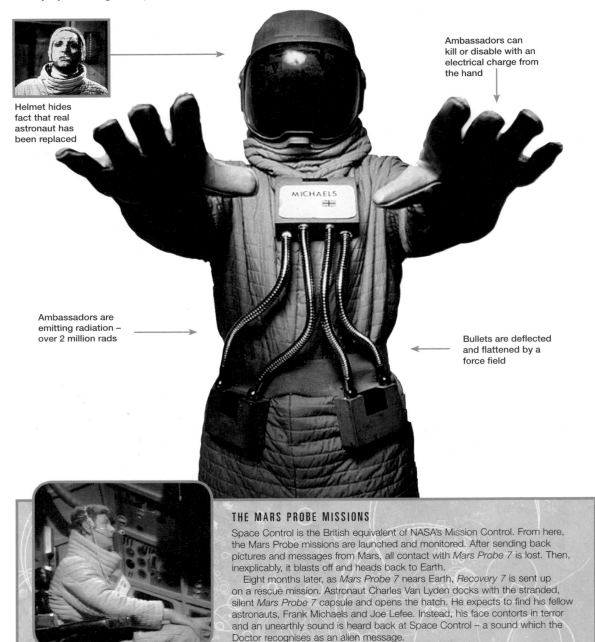

Helmet hides fact that real astronaut has been replaced

Ambassadors can kill or disable with an electrical charge from the hand

MICHAELS

Ambassadors are emitting radiation – over 2 million rads

Bullets are deflected and flattened by a force field

THE MARS PROBE MISSIONS

Space Control is the British equivalent of NASA's Mission Control. From here, the Mars Probe missions are launched and monitored. After sending back pictures and messages from Mars, all contact with *Mars Probe 7* is lost. Then, inexplicably, it blasts off and heads back to Earth.

Eight months later, as *Mars Probe 7* nears Earth, *Recovery 7* is sent up on a rescue mission. Astronaut Charles Van Lyden docks with the stranded, silent *Mars Probe 7* capsule and opens the hatch. He expects to find his fellow astronauts, Frank Michaels and Joe Lefee. Instead, his face contorts in terror and an unearthly sound is heard back at Space Control – a sound which the Doctor recognises as an alien message.

THE AMBASSADORS OF DEATH

On their return to Earth, the astronauts from *Mars Probe 7* and *Recovery 7* are kidnapped – but they are actually Ambassadors sent back by an alien race, and they need radiation to survive. General Carrington believes the aliens are evil and has arranged their kidnap, forcing them to commit murder. He plans to unmask one of the them on live television and turn public opinion against the well-intentioned aliens.

But the Doctor – who has visited the alien mothership in another rocket – and his friends from UNIT, find and free the other two Alien Ambassadors. They manage to stop Carrington's broadcast, and the Ambassadors are returned to their mothership.

Written by
David Whitaker
Featuring
the Third Doctor,
UNIT and Liz
First broadcast
21 March 1970 –
2 May 1970
7 episodes

THE ALIEN SHIP

The disc-shaped vessel is half a mile in diameter. It gives out radio impulses like those emitted by pulsars, and radio signals that jam NASA's cameras, so they can't get a picture of it.

The Doctor goes up in a rocket from Space Control to visit the ship. Inside, he finds an environment prepared for him. The interior of the ship is like a glowing orange cave. Here the real astronauts are being held in a mock-up of the reception centre at Space Control. They believe they are back on Earth waiting to be given the all-clear after decontamination.

ALIEN COMMUNICATION

Because the aliens' form of intelligence is so different from ours, they can only communicate by sending pictographic signals. Their first communication is a set of instructions, which the Doctor finally manages to decode. These instructions show him how to build a device with which to communicate with the Ambassadors.

General Carrington and his men use a similar device to force the aliens to do what he wants – threatening to withdraw the aliens' access to the radiation they need if they don't cooperate.

GENERAL CARRINGTON

General Carrington is the head of the newly formed Space Security Department. When he was an astronaut on *Mars Probe 6*, he met the aliens on Mars. His fellow astronaut (Jim Daniels) was killed by the aliens, who did not realise their touch could be fatal to humans. But Carrington blames them for the death and sets a trap for them.

Carrington believes that destroying the aliens is his moral duty, and will go to any lengths to 'save the Earth' – even killing scientist Lennox, and his own superior, Sir James Quinlan.

When ghostly, grey, translucent figures began to appear all round the world, there was panic. But after a while it became apparent that these figures were doing no harm, and people started to assume they must be ghosts. The figures were thought to be the spirits of loved ones who had died, returning to visit their former friends and families. But the truth was far more sinister ...

In a sense, these figures *were* from another world – but not the afterlife. They were coming through the void between universes, slipping through cracks created by a Void Ship. Their origin was a parallel Earth: similar to, yet in some ways very different from, our own. Once they arrived fully in our world, the millions of 'ghosts' could be seen for what they really were: Cybermen.

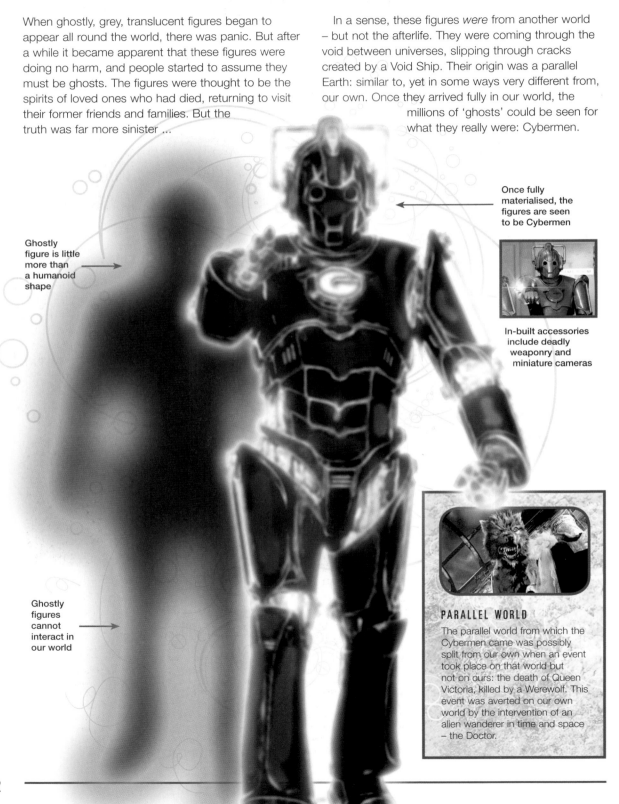

Once fully materialised, the figures are seen to be Cybermen

Ghostly figure is little more than a humanoid shape

In-built accessories include deadly weaponry and miniature cameras

Ghostly figures cannot interact in our world

PARALLEL WORLD

The parallel world from which the Cybermen came was possibly split from our own when an event took place on that world but not on ours: the death of Queen Victoria, killed by a Werewolf. This event was averted on our own world by the intervention of an alien wanderer in time and space – the Doctor.

ARMY OF GHOSTS

Jackie is convinced that she is being visited by the ghost of her father. Sure enough, the Doctor and Rose see a grey, translucent figure appear in her kitchen – and other 'ghosts' appear around the world. But they are being brought into existence by scientists at the Torchwood Institute. The Doctor is taken to Torchwood Tower, where he tries to persuade Yvonne Hartman that the experiments are damaging the very fabric of reality.

Meanwhile, Rose finds Mickey, who has returned from the parallel world where she last saw him. They investigate a mysterious Sphere that came through the Void. The ghosts materialise fully – as Cybermen – and then the Sphere opens and its occupants emerge: Daleks!

Written by
Russell T Davies
Featuring
the Tenth Doctor,
Rose and Mickey
First broadcast
1 July 2006
First of 2 episodes
(see page 25)

TORCHWOOD

The Torchwood Institute was established by Queen Victoria after she was nearly killed by a Werewolf, and was named after Torchwood House, where the incident happened. Its headquarters are in Canary Wharf Tower. It collects and investigates alien technology. Refusing to go metric, Torchwood upholds the tenets of the British Empire.

In charge is Yvonne Hartman, a woman so single-minded that she is able to resist her conversion into a Cyberman and fight back – doing her duty, for Queen and country.

THE GHOST SHIFT

Torchwood's experiments on the Sphere have opened the cracks between worlds, and the Cybermen can come through. The Sphere is a Void Ship, which has no real existence until the breach between reality and the Void is opened.

The Ghost Shift is the term Torchwood uses to describe the times when they energise the cracks between reality and the Void, to bring the 'ghosts' through. They do not realise how fragile reality has become, and continue their experiments, allowing the army of millions of Cybermen to materialise fully on Earth.

CYBER CONVERSION

The Cybermen have hidden conversion equipment inside Torchwood Tower, to 'upgrade' humans. They are ready to begin full conversions, and turn many Torchwood personnel into Cybermen, including Yvonne Hartman. They also partially convert some personnel before they reveal their presence. These people, conditioned with a brain implant attached to their earpods, are remote-controlled by the Cybermen. One of the partial converts is a young woman called Adeola – a cousin of the Doctor's future companion Martha Jones.

SCRIPTING 'ARMY OF GHOSTS'

Russell T Davies, lead writer and executive producer of **Doctor Who**, found the idea of pitching the Daleks and the Cybermen against each other irresistible. Despite the classic series running for so long, the two most popular of **Doctor Who**'s monstrous enemies had never met in battle. They featured together in 'guest' appearances in the same episode: in the Doctor's hallucinations in *The Mind of Evil*; and when the Doctor shows the Time Lords the evils he has fought, in *The War Games*. The closest they came to an encounter was in *The Five Doctors*, where a lone Dalek chases the First Doctor in the Death Zone on his home planet Gallifrey, while an army of Cybermen pursues his other incarnations.

It must have been daunting to bring the two super-monsters together, but Russell T Davies explains, in behind-the-scenes book *The Inside Story*, why he did it: 'It's irresistible to put them together; it's begging to be done.... Bronze and steel – they're just meant to clash. You've got to keep raising the stakes ... I wanted to create battleground Earth, where the human race is trapped in the middle of two giants scrapping. I always think that, in the mythology of the series, they're like gods ... These are two great big creatures from hell and they're sent into hell at the end ... For there to be hell on Earth, it means Daleks versus Cybermen, and the stakes have got to be that high for the Doctor to lose Rose at the end ... for the ending to be truly cataclysmic.'

CYBER INVASION

Although the invading Cybermen seem frighteningly real, many were computer-generated. It is typical of the quality of the effects provided by The Mill that it's impossible to tell which are which.

The ghosts were also created by The Mill, based on shots of actors in black suits against green screens. The scenes were shot without the ghosts and they were added afterwards. When they materialised fully, these figures were blended with the outlines of the Cybermen.

SECRET INVASION

In the original script, Adeola's frightening encounter with the Cybermen did not reveal who had actually infiltrated Torchwood Tower:

```
The shadow is silent,
unmoving. Just one more
curtain of thick polythene
between them; maybe, this
close, the shape around
its head visible; a
handle-type structure ...
She reaches out, she parts
the polythene ...

HIGH ANGLE POV looking down at Adeola. And she just
stares up. Rigid. In shock. Hold.
```

It was not until the Doctor found the cordoned-off area that they were revealed:

```
A shadow's hand reaches up. The edge of the hand slices
through the tight polythene, top to bottom, like a knife
through butter, the metal hand protruding through -

THE DOCTOR
Cybermen.

And the CYBERMEN step through!
```

THE CARRIONITES

The ancient and awful Carrionites – from the Fourteen Stars of the Rexel Planetary Configuration – developed a science that was based on words instead of numbers. While humanity followed the mathematical route, creating formulae to explain the universe, the Carrionites pursued a form of science that exploits the power of language. To those who do not understand the distinction, it seems that the Carrionites chant spells.

Long ago, the Eternals – beings who exist in the eternity outside ephemeral time – found the 'spell' (the right word) to banish the Carrionites into Deep Darkness. It was thought they could never return, but the death of Shakespeare's young son released such grief in the playwright that this brought back three of the Carrionites. In Elizabethan London, they set about using their 'magic' to have Shakespeare's words release all the Carrionites to feed on the world.

← Evil eyes

← Hooked nose

← Wrinkled, wizened skin

Hag-like appearance →

THE SHAKESPEARE CODE

The Doctor takes Martha to a play at the newly opened Globe Theatre in Elizabethan London. They meet Shakespeare, who is completing his sequel to *Love's Labour's Lost* – called *Love's Labour's Won*. But he has fallen under the influence of three Carrionites, who are using his powerful words, coupled with the shape of the Globe Theatre, to create a 'spell' that will release the other Carrionites from the Deep Darkness.

The Doctor encourages Shakespeare to rework the play's ending and the words of power are turned on the Carrionites, banishing them again. After some initial confusion, the audience expresses its appreciation of the one and only, effects-laden performance of *Love's Labour's Won*.

Written by
Gareth Roberts
Featuring
the Tenth Doctor
and Martha
First broadcast
7 April 2007
1 episode

WILLIAM SHAKESPEARE

Widely regarded as the greatest poet and playwright in history, Shakespeare is in his mid-thirties and at the height of his success. He is a man so talented that his words can free the Carrionites; so grief-stricken by the death of his son that the Carrionites can twist his emotions to their need. He is perceptive enough to realise where – and when – the Doctor and Martha are from, but is not above 'borrowing' words that he overhears. One word of the Doctor's that appeals to him is 'Sycorax' – the name he will give to the witch-mother in *The Tempest*.

DNA REPLICATION

One of the techniques the Carrionites use, which seems close to witchcraft, is DNA replication. From a small amount of a person's DNA they can bind a doll-like figurine to that person: whatever happens to the doll, happens to the person.

Using this technique, Lilith kills Lynley, Master of the Revels, when he threatens to stop the performance of *Love's Labour's Won*. She plunges the doll into a bucket of water, and so Lynley drowns. Later she uses the doll to make Shakespeare write the final scene of the play, and to try to kill the Doctor.

THE GLOBE

The Carrionites have manipulated Peter Streete, who designed the Globe Theatre, to create a building to their specifications. The result is fourteen-sided, amplifying the words of power at the end of the play. His job done, he is driven mad by the Carrionites and consigned to Bedlam.

The Globe opened in 1599. It burned down in 1613, but was rebuilt. Puritans (who opposed the existence of theatres) demolished it in 1644. The Globe was recreated at London's Bear Garden and officially opened again in 1997.

A MUSE OF FIRE

The Shakespeare Code was written by Gareth Roberts – an established and talented television writer who has worked on series from **Randall and Hopkirk (Deceased)** to **Coronation Street**, and co-wrote the first of **The Sarah Jane Adventures** with Russell T Davies.

Gareth Roberts is well known to **Doctor Who** fans for his recent novels: *Only Human* featuring the Ninth Doctor, and the Quick Reads Tenth Doctor title *I Am a Dalek*. He also wrote a number of very popular classic **Doctor Who** novels. Here, he explains something of the Carrionites background and history:

'The Fourteen Stars of the Rexel Planetary Configuration have been a mystery since the dawn of understanding in the universe. Legend has it that the Rexel stars are a prison door, sealed billions of years in the past, keeping the Carrionites in Deep Darkness.

'The Carrionites, legendarily, ate their own husbands and children. They are said to have developed a malevolent science of their own – using shapes, words, numbers and names to effect their attacks on hundreds of their neighbouring planets back at the dawn of time. They used the grief and suffering of others to enhance this science – which to us is indistinguishable from magic.

'The Eternals are said to have banished the Carrionites into Deep Darkness. It took the grief of a genius – Shakespeare, driven nearly insane by the death of one of his children – to allow a small group of them, led by Lilith, back into our universe, to plot the return of the others.'

Above: Some very special effects at the Globe Theatre.
Opposite (top): A previously undiscovered Shakespeare manuscript.
Opposite (bottom): The Doctor and Martha at the Globe Theatre.

From out night's parted veil vaunt wretched hags,
Whose former empery of blood and bone
Consigned to Deep Darkness, complot to steal
Th'impressions of our fantasies in words
Thereby to blot out realm, the world, and all.
Vile bounded power awak'd by boundless grief
Made form by poet's trumpeted renown
Takes shape from shapes poured subtly in the ear
Of lunatics, to wreck the globe from 'Globe'.
Yet providence provides two saviours near
The Doctor and his incomparable maid
(Their voyages not hemmed in by
space nor time)
They know a curse to curse this
damned spite
With its foul title, baleful
Carrionite.

William Shakespeare
(channelled by Gareth Roberts)

ALL THE WORLD'S A STAGE

Although all the action of *The Shakespeare Code* takes place in London, the **Doctor Who** production team used a variety of locations and techniques to recreate the Tudor city. Extensive use was made of the recreated Globe Theatre, but the Elephant Inn, where Shakespeare stays, and the Carrionites' dwelling on Allhallows Street were found elsewhere.

One very useful location was the Lord Leycester Hospital on the main street in Warwick. Despite being on a busy modern road, the building has been used before for Elizabethan dramas, and provided an authentic backdrop. The final effect of placing the building in the heart of a medieval cityscape of London was achieved by The Mill, who supplied the digital painting of the background and city.

The Mill also created the impressive finale, as the Carrionites arrive in force at the Globe and fly round the audience like ethereal spirits (*above*). The wizened, hag-like figures of Mothers Doomfinger and Bloodtide, and their 'daughter' Lilith when in witch-form (*below*), were achieved using prosthetic make-up supplied by Neill Gorton and Millennium FX.

This page: Initial concept artwork (middle) and the final digital matte paintings (top and bottom) for the medieval cityscape. Note how Lord Leycester Hospital is incorporated (left concept and bottom matte). Opposite: Original design concepts for the Carrionites (far left and top) and the Carrionites themselves.

THE CELESTIAL TOYMAKER

Although he dresses like an imposing, medieval Chinese nobleman, the Toymaker is an incredibly powerful being who has lived for thousands of years. He spends his time playing games. If he loses, the price he pays is the destruction of his world, but he is powerful enough to rebuild it. (His winning opponent is destroyed with the world.) If his opponents lose, they are added to the domain as his toys. The Doctor calls him '... a power for evil. He manipulates people and makes them into his playthings.'

The Toymaker is probably immortal

Toymaker turns people into toys

Traditional Chinese clothes

THE TOYMAKER'S GAMES:
The games the Toymaker forces his opponents to play include:
· **The Trilogic Game** – see page 23
· **Blind Man's Buff** – with cheating dolls
· **Musical Chairs** – with chairs that kill whoever sits down on them
· **Hopscotch** – across a lethal, electrified floor

The Doctor meets the Celestial Toymaker and his clowns Joey and Clara.

THE CELESTIAL TOYMAKER

The TARDIS materialises in the domain of the Toymaker, who turns people into his playthings. The Toymaker makes the Doctor invisible and forces him to play the Trilogic Game. In order to escape, the Doctor and his companions must defeat the Toymaker and his toys in a variety of games. If they lose, they will be added to the Toymaker's collection, but if they win, the Toymaker's domain will be destroyed – along with the winning players.

The Doctor imitates the Toymaker's voice to make the winning move in the Trilogic Game from the safety of the TARDIS – and so he and his companions survive the destruction.

Written by
Brian Hayles
Featuring
the First Doctor,
Steven and Dodo
First broadcast
2 April 1966 –
23 April 1966
4 episodes

PLAYTHINGS

All the Toymaker's subjects are, in actual fact, toys. He takes two dolls from their dolls' house and they become Joey and Clara. After they lose their game against Dodo and Steven, Joey and Clara become dolls again.

The Toymaker threatens to break Sergeant Rugg and Mrs Wiggs the cook like a stack of plates. Other playthings include a robot, naughty schoolboy Cyril, and the Hearts family – the King, Queen and Knave – who are really playing cards.

THE TRILOGIC GAME

The Trilogic Game consists of a pyramid made of numbered layers that form the playing pieces. There are three points, A, B and C, on the board arranged in a triangle. Similar to the game 'Towers of Hanoi' (played with circular pieces), the player has to move the pyramid from point A to point C, moving one layer at a time, and never placing a larger piece on top of a smaller piece.

An added complication is that the new pyramid has to be completed at position C in exactly 1023 moves.

RETURN VISIT

The Toymaker says that the Doctor has visited his domain before, but did not stay long enough to play any of the games. This may be because the Doctor has heard of the Toymaker, too.

'You and your games are quite notorious,' the Doctor tells him. 'You draw people here like a spider does to flies … and should they lose the games they play, you condemn them to become your toys forever.'

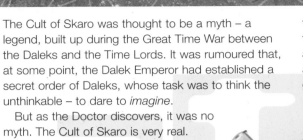

The Cult of Skaro was thought to be a myth – a legend, built up during the Great Time War between the Daleks and the Time Lords. It was rumoured that, at some point, the Dalek Emperor had established a secret order of Daleks, whose task was to think the unthinkable – to dare to *imagine*.

But as the Doctor discovers, it was no myth. The Cult of Skaro is very real. More important even than the Emperor,

the Cult of Skaro is made up of four Daleks who tried to think like the enemy, to get inside enemy minds and predict their strategies so as to give the Daleks an advantage in their wars. These Daleks have even given themselves names – as a part of becoming enough like the enemy to predict and counter their actions. They are called Daleks Sec, Thay, Jast and Caan.

Dalek Thay

Dalek Jast

Dalek Sec – leader of the Cult of Skaro

Dalek Caan

DOOMSDAY

Millions of Cybermen have materialised from an alternative Earth, and four Daleks emerge from their Void Ship. The Cybermen suggest an alliance, but the Daleks – the legendary Cult of Skaro – see them as pests and the two join battle. The Daleks win easily and open their Genesis Ark: hundreds of Daleks emerge in the skies over London, so the Doctor re-opens the Void. Contaminated with 'void material', Daleks and Cybermen are sucked back into the empty space between universes.

But Rose, her mum and Mickey are trapped on the parallel Earth. To save both universes, the Doctor must close the holes into the Void. After a tearful farewell, he and Rose part, never to see each other again.

Written by
Russell T Davies
Featuring
the Tenth Doctor,
Rose and Mickey
First broadcast
8 July 2006
Second of 2 episodes
(see page 13)

THE GREAT TIME WAR

Long ago, the Time Lords of Gallifrey tried to prevent the Daleks from ever existing by sending the Doctor back in time to stop them being created. When the Daleks discovered what the Time Lords had tried to do, they retaliated, and a full-scale war erupted within the Time Vortex, and beyond.

When the war was over, a single survivor walked through the carnage of Gallifrey and Skaro – the Time Lord who had brought the war to its terrible end: the Doctor. Although he did not know it at the time, the Daleks had also survived.

THE VOID

When the Daleks realised they couldn't defeat the Time Lords without being destroyed themselves, the Cult of Skaro devised a Void Ship to hide between the universes, waiting for the war to end.

The Void is nowhere, a place that doesn't exist. The TARDIS travelled through it when it took the Doctor, Rose and Mickey to an Earth where the Cybermen were being created. It fell through a crack that the Void Ship had left in the fabric of the universe. The Cybermen used similar cracks to come through to our own world.

THE GENESIS ARK

During the Great Time War, the Time Lords took many Daleks prisoner and locked them in a huge prison. But the Time Lords know how to fit enormous spaces into tiny containers – just like the Doctor's TARDIS – so the prison was contained inside a large casket.

The Daleks captured the casket, and they hid it in the void between universes, together with the Cult of Skaro. They called it the Genesis Ark because it was their future, their survival – a vast army of Daleks waiting to emerge once the war was over.

DOOMSDAY DAWNS

The climactic, shocking end of *Army of Ghosts* and the beginning of *Doomsday* see the mysterious Void Ship open to reveal its contents. The audience – along with Rose and Mickey – holds its breath. What will be inside? Yet more Cybermen? The Cyber Controller? Something even more terrifying … but what could be more terrifying?

The answer arrives in the form of the four Daleks that rise from the Sphere and advance on Rose and Mickey.

This sequence is all the more impressive when you consider that none of the main elements actually existed in the studio. The Sphere itself was created as a computer-generated image (CGI) by effects house The Mill. Although the Daleks that advance across the Sphere room are 'real', the first sight of them rising from the Void Ship is another CGI. The combination of these computer-generated elements, live-action Daleks, and the reactions of Rose, Mickey and Doctor Rajesh Singh, creates one of the most terrifying cliffhangers ever in **Doctor Who**.

Top: The Void Ship opens to reveal the Daleks.
Above: On set for Doomsday.
Opposite, top right: The Doctor and Dalek Sec rehearse their lines.

THE FINAL END

More Dalek props were used for *Doomsday* than any previous story. Even though *The Parting of the Ways* saw an army of thousands of Daleks, there were only three Dalek props used in that story. For *Doomsday*, four Daleks were used, with CGI again providing the thousands of Daleks seen swarming above London.

The original Dalek prop used in the episode *Dalek* was repainted black to become Dalek Sec. The design department had tried out different colour schemes on toy Daleks before deciding exactly how the black Dalek would look. The other Daleks in the Cult of Skaro – Dalek Thay, Dalek Jast and Dalek Caan – retained the bronze colour scheme of the previous stories. Each of the Daleks had its own identity mark below the eye stalk; all unique, but similar, to show they were part of the Cult of Skaro.

Reproduced below are some of the storyboards used to work out the sequences showing the destruction of the Daleks as they are sucked back into the Void.

13.68.20   DALEKS PASS LEVERS AS THEY ARE SUCKED INTO VOID.

13.74.03

13.68.18   DALEKS GET SUCKED TO THE LEFT. PAN WITH THEM.

13.68.19   DALEKS GET SUCKED IN THROUGH WINDOW.

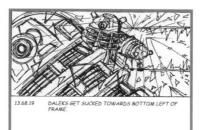

13.68.19   DALEKS GET SUCKED TOWARDS BOTTOM LEFT OF FRAME.

13.72.01   10 DALEKS HOVERING AND FIRING SUDDENLY

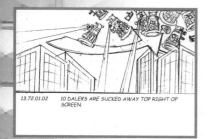

13.72.01.02   10 DALEKS ARE SUCKED AWAY TOP RIGHT OF SCREEN.

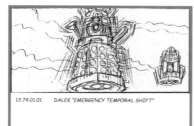

13.74.01.01   DALEK "EMERGENCY TEMPORAL SHIFT"

13.74.01.02   DALEK DISSAPEARS

Porcine hair

Creature used to be human

Pig-like snout and features

Enlarged ears

PIG MEN

Experimenting with the genetic structure of the human race, the Daleks created the Pig Men. They took ordinary human beings – such as the unfortunate Laszlo, a stagehand at the Laurenzi Theatre – and turned them into creatures that were half-human, half-pig.

The Daleks also brainwashed the creatures they had created, so that the Pig Men became their unquestioning servants, ready to steal more humans for them: humans that were needed for another purpose – the Final Experiment.

HUMAN-DALEKS

Unable to grow new Dalek embryos, the Cult of Skaro turned instead to the greatest resource that Earth had to offer them: its people.

In the secret caverns beneath the Empire State Building, the Daleks are storing over a thousand transgenically processed humans. Their minds have been wiped, and – held close to death – they have been conditioned to obey; to be like the Daleks. The humans are waiting to be reborn as new and deadly creatures. A massive blast of gamma radiation from a solar flare will splice human and Dalek genetic codes and waken the army – an army of Human-Daleks ready to conquer Earth.

Dalek brain remains intact →

Dalek and human fused together →

Features are reminiscent of original Dalek creature →

← Single blue eye

DALEK SEC HYBRID

Having tried – and failed – to create new Dalek embryos, the Cult of Skaro adopts another plan. As well as genetically adapting human beings to become Dalek-like, Dalek Sec is genetically bonded with a human being. The human chosen is Mr Diagoras – the man in charge of completing the Empire State Building, who has been working for the Daleks for a while.

Using a chromatin solution, Mr Diagoras is pushed into the flesh of the Dalek Sec creature, and the two become one. In order to survive, the Dalek species must evolve and experience life outside their shells – the children of Skaro must walk again.

DALEKENIUM CONDUCTOR

The Dalek plan to resurrect over a thousand processed people as Human-Daleks depends on the channelling of a vast amount of power. To achieve this, the Daleks have created a conductor on the top of the new Empire State Building that will collect and provide gamma radiation from a massive solar flare. The conductor is made up of several panels taken from the casing of Dalek Thay.

DALEKS IN MANHATTAN and EVOLUTION OF THE DALEKS

Written by
Helen Raynor
Featuring
the Tenth Doctor
and Martha
First broadcast
21 April 2007 –
28 April 2007
2 episodes

The Doctor and Martha arrive in 1930s New York and discover that the sinister Mr Diagoras is in league with the Cult of Skaro, who have escaped to New York and are using humans converted into pig-like creatures as slaves. Having failed to create an army of 'real' Daleks, they are planning to convert people into Human-Daleks, and have a vast army hidden beneath the Empire State Building. When energy from a solar flare strikes a conductor installed in the building, the army will awaken.

But Dalek Sec genetically bonds with Mr Diagoras in an effort to evolve into a super-Dalek. Will the Dalek Sec Hybrid realise that the Dalek way is flawed? And can the Doctor stop the Daleks in time?

HOOVERVILLE

The American boom of the 1920s came to an abrupt end with the Wall Street Crash in 1929: suddenly, shares were worthless. Thousands of people lost their jobs. In New York many of those who were evicted from their homes ended up in Central Park, where a vast shantytown was set up. It was, rather sarcastically, called Hooverville, after US president Herbert Clark Hoover. When the Doctor and Martha arrive they find Solomon keeping the people there in order, though Mr Diagoras is recruiting for Dalek slaves among the dispossessed.

THE EMPIRE STATE BUILDING

Completed in 1931, New York's 102-floor Empire State Building was the highest building in the world until 1972. The distinctive mast where the Daleks place their Dalekenium conductor was originally designed as a mooring post for airships. But the architects were not to know that construction of the building would be taken over by the Cult of Skaro, working through the unprincipled Mr Diagoras.

The Daleks also constructed a secret base and laboratory beneath the structure where they stored their Human-Dalek army ready to be activated.

THE FINAL EXPERIMENT

Believing themselves to be the last four Daleks in existence, the Cult of Skaro are determined to think unlike any other Daleks. But the audaciousness of Dalek Sec's plan to evolve the Dalek race by bonding human and Dalek flesh worries the other Daleks and they warn Dalek Sec not to proceed with it.

Ultimately, they are right: the Dalek Sec Hybrid is corrupted by his humanity, and betrays them. But the Daleks are not defeated – not while one single Dalek remains alive…

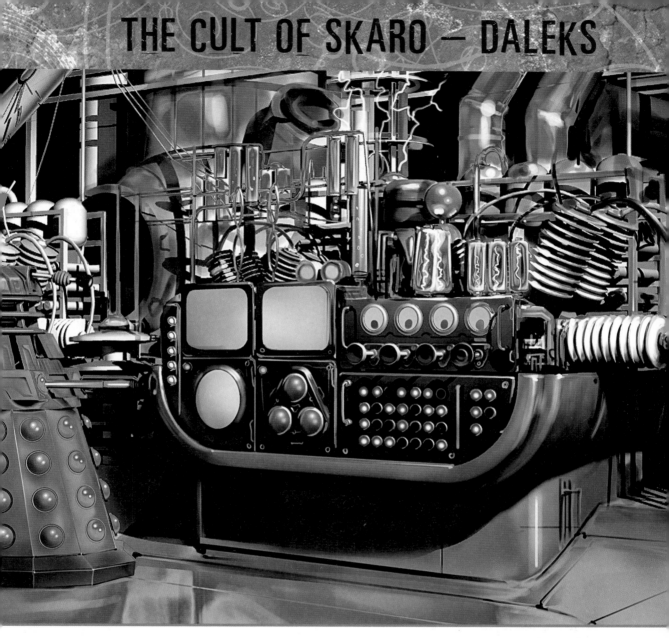

DALEK MILITARY COMPUTER

Installed in their transgenic laboratory, deep below the Empire State Building, the Daleks' Military Computer is ready to coordinate their war strategy as they unleash their army of converted Human-Daleks. The computer is operated by a Dalek that is plugged directly into the systems and becomes one with the computer. Through the computer, the Dalek can monitor the Human-Dalek army and issue orders directly to it.

The system was originally designed so that Dalek Sec – the leader of the Cult of Skaro – would operate it. But after Dalek Sec is genetically bonded with Mr Diagoras and begins to doubt underlying Dalek philosophy, the other Daleks overrule his authority and Dalek Caan assumes responsibility for all military strategy and operations.

When the other Daleks – Thay and Jast – are destroyed, Dalek Caan is able to draw on enough power, possibly from the Military Computer itself, to activate its emergency temporal shift and escape from the Doctor and his allies.

EPIC ELEMENTS

Daleks in Manhattan was written by one of **Doctor Who**'s script editors: Helen Raynor. Although more used to working on other

writers' scripts, Helen has written for both radio and television, including episodes of the **Doctor Who** spin-off series **Torchwood**.

Helen explained how she devised the elements of the story and brought them together into an epic struggle for survival:

'The Empire State Building was a gift, and it helped me settle on the 1930 date pretty early on. It's iconic, it was the tallest building in the world and there was enough mystery and controversy surrounding the "mooring mast" at the top to spark my curiosity. Being the highest building, the Empire State itself was in effect the tallest lightning conductor in Manhattan. Also, in 1931, the year it opened, Boris Karloff's creature in *Frankenstein* terrorised audiences by lurching into life after being animated by lightning ... Irresistibly juicy ingredients. I always wanted the whole thing to feel like a family-show take on 1930s horror films – everything from the shadowy sewers to the "mad scientist" transgenic lab could have come from a Universal Pictures Film.

'Russell T Davies talked about using a theatre, and showgirls – which in itself is a bit *King Kong* – and the minute I thought of a theatre, I thought of *Phantom of the Opera* (Lon Chaney's *Phantom* film was released only a few years earlier, in 1925). Which gave me poor faithful Laszlo – half-man, half-pig. He has Russell T Davies to thank for his survival – I originally killed him off, in a scene of indulgent, heartrending tragedy, which didn't sit well in our optimistic series. It would have been a right downer for kids at Saturday teatime.

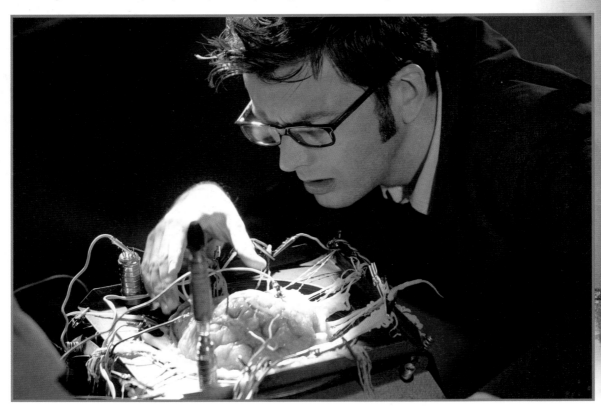

THE CULT OF SKARO — DALEKS

'1930 gave me a very specific time in the Depression as well. Just one year after the Wall Street Crash, while America was still in deep shock – before Roosevelt's "New Deal" was even a glimmer of light on the horizon. Ours is a family-show take on the Central Park "Hooverville" – the real thing would have been much more brutal. But it still has the feel of real desperation – the need to survive. A theme which fed right into the heart of the Dalek story....'

Top: The Mill's finished, computer-generated Hooverville.
Above: The initial concept for Hooverville.
Opposite (main pic): The Doctor examines a Dalek genetic experiment.

BRINGING THE DALEKS TO LIFE

As well as New York in 1930, the Empire State Building, Pig Men and the theatre, there was something else that Helen Raynor had to include in her script. The executive producers of **Doctor Who**, Julie Gardner and Russell T Davies, shocked Helen by asking her to write a Dalek story:

'It was one of the hardest secrets I've ever had to keep (from March 2006 to Christmas, thank you very much).

'The story started like they all do: a big chat with Russell T Davies, where we talked about the Daleks and Nature, Destiny, Survival, Evolution, Imagination, Heresy – all key ingredients in the final mix. Daleks come with a big history, and an almost mythical status, which makes them amazing, but pretty daunting, to write for.

'So I went back to basics. What did I remember about them as a child? Why were they so scary? The grating voice, the remorseless onward glide – all the physical manifestations of that will to power, that single-mindedness, that drive to exterminate everything else – writing them really made me appreciate how perfect their design is. They look like what they are. And they certainly look at home in 1930 – military Art Deco, that's a Dalek for you.

'The "back to basics" approach took me back to all of the Dalek stories, but especially *Genesis of the Daleks*, which

tells the story of their creation. It's a brilliant story about survival, and the need to become strong, removing human weaknesses; human emotion. What we were writing now was a companion piece to that, in a way – the need to survive, but now to contemplate reversing the process. Because the Dalek conundrum in these episodes is: If humans are weak, and we are strong – why are there millions of humans, and four of us?

'The origin of the Dalek race was genetic mutation, and it's the way to their future. So says the Dalek Sec Hybrid – a prophet and orator, and every inch a match for the Doctor. Together, they make a plan that could end the genocidal wars of the Daleks. If only ...'

Top: The Doctor confronts the Daleks.
Above: Design painting of the Dalek laboratory.
Opposite (top): Design painting of the unfinished Empire State Building.
Opposite (main): Design for Dalek Thay's replacement panels.

HUMANISING A DALEK

The task of designing and creating the features of the Dalek Sec Hybrid was given to Neill Gorton's Millennium FX company. The starting point was a sketch of how the final creature might look – retaining some human features, including the mouth, but also incorporating a large amount of Dalek anatomy. The single Dalek eye was made more human – and was blue, to echo the colour of the Dalek machine's eye stalk.

The next stage was to create a clay sculpture of the head, and from this the final prosthetic and animatronic components were made for the actor, Eric Loren, to wear. He was able to use his own mouth to speak, but other movement, including that of the tentacles, was achieved using radio control.

The head was in several sections – make-up pieces glued on for the mouth, a balaclava-like mask for the neck, and an easily removable head piece for the brain and tentacles.

The final result is a startling, very alien creature that is obviously Dalek, but also disconcertingly human.

Top: Sculpting a clay model of the head. Above left: Fitting the head on set.
Above right: A picture of the clay model, with tentacles and eye painted on to show the finished effect.

Lord of Darkness and Eater of Worlds, the Destroyer is a demon-like creature summoned by the sorceress Morgaine when she thinks she is in danger of losing her battle against the Doctor and his friends. She calls the Destroyer into existence in our world.

Morgaine has the Destroyer chained with silver, which burns the creature, keeping it powerless. But Morgaine calls the Doctor's bluff and frees the Destroyer so it can claim the world to devour. As the world explodes round the Destroyer, the Doctor's old friend the Brigadier kills it with silver bullets.

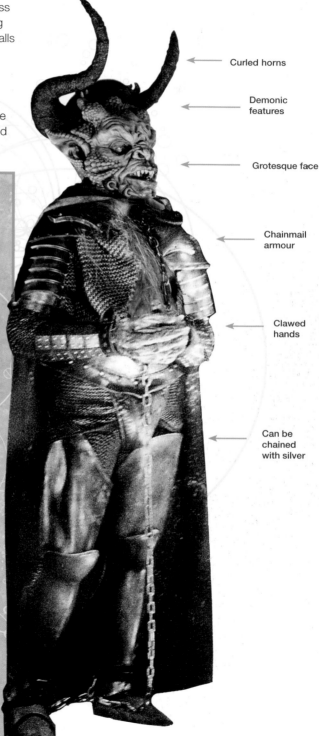

Curled horns

Demonic features

Grotesque face

Chainmail armour

Clawed hands

Can be chained with silver

MORGAINE

Morgaine is from a parallel world where a medieval culture developed technology alongside magic, and the legends of King Arthur are actual fact. Although he's unsure how, the Doctor – in another incarnation – is Merlin, and Morgaine is sworn to destroy him.

Morgaine of the Faye, the Sunkiller – Dominator of the Thirteen Worlds and Battle Queen of the S'rax – also wants revenge on Arthur, unaware that he is already dead. She demands to face Arthur in single combat – but he was killed over a thousand years earlier in the final battle. His 'body' is actually an empty suit of armour, with a note the future Doctor has written to himself in the helmet.

Knights from another dimension clash in our world.

BATTLEFIELD

Written by
Ben Aaronovitch
Featuring
the Seventh Doctor,
UNIT and Ace
First broadcast
6 September 1989 –
27 September 1989
4 episodes

Knights in armour arrive from a parallel reality where technology and magic exist together and the legends of King Arthur are fact. Mordred battles against his enemy Ancelyn, and summons his mother, Morgaine, to help him. The Doctor and Ace find a UNIT convoy stranded beside Lake Vortigern. Under the lake is Arthur's spaceship, linked to the shore by an ancient tunnel that opens in response to the Doctor's voice. On board the ship is Arthur's body; he has been dead for centuries.

Morgaine tries to gain the upper hand by unleashing the powerful Destroyer to devour the world. But Brigadier Lethbridge-Stewart kills the creature with silver bullets, and Morgaine surrenders to the UNIT forces.

UNIT

A secret organisation that the Doctor worked for in his third incarnation, UNIT is responsible for investigating unusual and alien threats to Earth. UNIT's headquarters is in Geneva, and each country is responsible for providing military personnel to staff their local contingents.

The UK section of UNIT is now commanded by Brigadier Winifred Bambera, following the retirement of UNIT's first UK commanding officer, Brigadier Lethbridge-Stewart.

BRIGADIER LETHBRIDGE-STEWART

Brigadier Alistair Lethbridge-Stewart worked as a colonel with the Second Doctor, fighting against deadly Yeti in the Underground. When UNIT was formed, Lethbridge-Stewart was promoted to brigadier and put in command of the UK section. He worked with the Doctor again to defeat the Cybermen.

Throughout his third incarnation, the Doctor assisted the Brigadier, battling against misguided scientists, Daleks, and the renegade Time Lord known as the Master. Now the Brigadier has retired and lives with his wife Doris.

BESSIE

One of the conditions on which the Doctor originally agreed to work for UNIT was that he should have a car. He chose a yellow vintage car, which he called Bessie and modified extensively. Bessie has an anti-theft device that 'glues' the potential thief to the car, inertia-absorbing brakes, a 'Super-Drive' option for high-speed travel, and can even be operated by remote control.

Bessie's number plate was WHO1 throughout the Doctor's UNIT years, but for her reappearance in *Battlefield* this has been changed to WHO7.

CREATING THE DESTROYER

The Destroyer was made by freelance effects designers Susan Moore and Stephen Mansfield with additional help from Robert Allsopp (who made the special, lightweight horns).

In the original script, the Destroyer started out as 'an ordinary, rather aristocratic human man, impeccably dressed'. But when he is unleashed by Morgaine, the 'man' grows horns and talons and turns into a gigantic creature 'with glowing green eyes and hide-like armour'. But this would have taken too much time and money to achieve, and so the Destroyer appeared as a demonic creature right the way through the story.

Moore and Mansfield had already sculpted a demon-like head as an example of the work they could do, and, impressed with this, the production team for *Battlefield* asked them to create the Destroyer based on the design. Some changes were made to make the design more practical as a mask, which actor Marek Anton would have to wear to say his lines, and a new version was sculpted in clay.

From this, moulds were made and the final mask was cast in foam latex, which was then fitted over a fibreglass shell that the actor could wear. Cables attached to the inside of the mask controlled the snarling mouth and creasing brow of the creature,

with the mechanism hidden beneath the Destroyer's cloak for the actor to operate.

In the final episode of *Battlefield*, when the Destroyer is shot by the Brigadier, its head explodes. For this effect, a wax copy was made of the head (from the original mould for the mask). In fact, four wax heads were made, so the explosion could be filmed several times if necessary. It was actually shot twice, once in the studio and once at the effects workshop.

Top: Stephen Mansfield working on the Destroyer.
Above: Fitting the Destroyer's horns.
Right: The impressive final creature.

THE EMPRESS OF THE RACNOSS

The Racnoss are huge creatures that came from the Dark Times, billions of years ago. They were born hungry and devoured everything – even whole planets. The Fledgeling Empires went to war against the Racnoss and wiped them out – or so they thought. One Racnoss survived ... the Empress.

In hibernation, she drifted in her Webstar spaceship to the very edge of space. There, awakened at last from her slumbers, she sought the last of her subjects and found they had escaped into the orbit of a new star, just as its solar system was forming. A planet had formed round the Racnoss eggs: Earth.

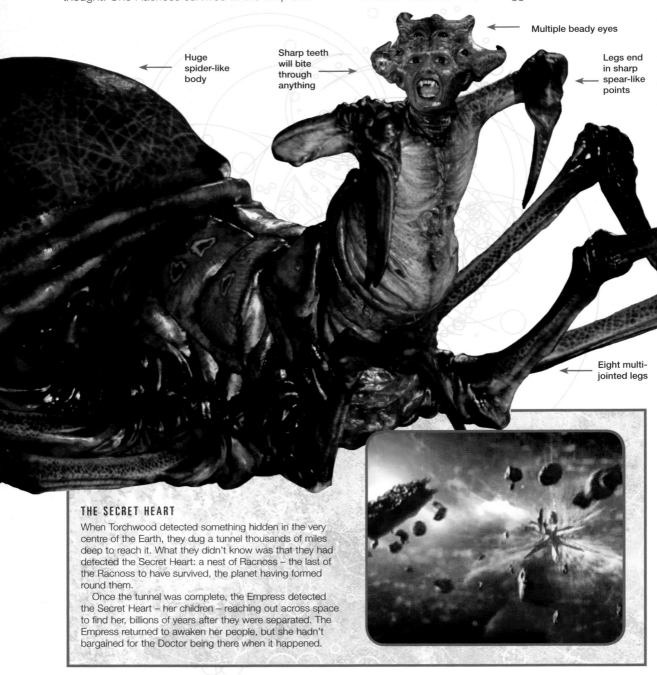

Huge spider-like body

Sharp teeth will bite through anything

Multiple beady eyes

Legs end in sharp spear-like points

Eight multi-jointed legs

THE SECRET HEART

When Torchwood detected something hidden in the very centre of the Earth, they dug a tunnel thousands of miles deep to reach it. What they didn't know was that they had detected the Secret Heart: a nest of Racnoss – the last of the Racnoss to have survived, the planet having formed round them.

Once the tunnel was complete, the Empress detected the Secret Heart – her children – reaching out across space to find her, billions of years after they were separated. The Empress returned to awaken her people, but she hadn't bargained for the Doctor being there when it happened.

THE RUNAWAY BRIDE

Donna Noble is at her own wedding when she suddenly fades away ... and reappears inside the TARDIS. The Doctor realises that Donna is being chased by the Pilot Fish Roboforms he encountered before the Sycorax invasion – again disguised as sinister Santas.

Donna has been dosed with deadly Huon particles so that she will revive the dormant children of the Empress of the Racnoss, who now controls the Roboforms. But the Doctor uses explosive baubles from the deadly Christmas trees to flood the Empress's underground base, drowning the Racnoss. The Empress appears to die when her Webstar spaceship is destroyed by an armoured tank.

Written by
Russell T Davies
Featuring
the Tenth Doctor
and Donna
First broadcast
25 December 2006
A 60-minute
Christmas Special

DONNA NOBLE

Life seems to be coming together for Donna Noble. She has a good job at security firm H. C. Clements, and is about to marry her fiancé Lance. But Donna has been dosed with deadly Huon particles to turn her into the key to the rebirth of the hideous Racnoss.

Transported to the TARDIS, Donna needs the Doctor's help to discover the truth – and defeat the Empress. Chased by sinister Santas and attacked by deadly Christmas trees, Donna decides to stay at home rather than accept the Doctor's invitation to travel with him.

LANCE BENNETT

Head of Human Resources at H. C. Clements, Lance has formed an alliance with the Empress of the Racnoss. He will provide the key to release her children – and that key is Donna, dosed with Huon particles in her coffee. Lance even agrees to marry Donna to make sure she cannot escape from him.

The Empress has promised to show Lance the universe, but she betrays him – using him, instead of Donna, as the key, force-feeding him Huon liquid and dropping him through a shaft to the centre of the Earth.

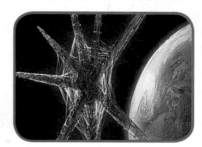

THE WEBSTAR

The spaceships of the Racnoss are their Webstars – giant star-shaped structures of intricate web material. As the Empress prepares for her children to emerge from the centre of the Earth, where they are in hibernation inside their own ancient Webstar, her Webstar descends. It shoots out bolts of deadly energy that will reduce the human race to nothing more than food. The Empress's children will be hungry when they emerge ...

But the Empress has used all the ship's energy to release the children and it is shot down by blasts from a tank.

THE PILOT FISH ROBOFORMS

The Doctor first encountered the Roboforms soon after he regenerated into his current form, and described them as 'pilot fish' arriving in the wake of the Sycorax spaceship (*The Christmas Invasion*).

Exactly where the Pilot Fish Roboforms come from is still not clear, but they seem to crave energy – power to keep them going. They are controlled remotely and have now come under the influence of the Empress of the Racnoss. She uses the Roboforms, still disguised as a Santa band, to hunt for Donna, but the Doctor is able to override her control.

Santa mask hides robotic features beneath

Red camouflage disguise suit for concealment

HERE COMES SINISTER SANTA

Unlike the Santa masks used in *The Christmas Invasion* – which were made to look as if the Roboforms were wearing false beards – the masks for *The Runaway Bride* were a single, fibre-glass piece that was big enough to fit over the new gold-coloured robot heads worn by the actor. The heads were also made from fibre-glass.

DEADLY CHRISTMAS TREES

Once again – as in *The Christmas Invasion* – the Doctor is menaced by Roboform Christmas trees. Placed at Donna's wedding reception, presumably by Lance with the help of the Santa Roboforms, these trees are decorated with exploding baubles.

Baubles and decorations are deadly explosives

Leaves are miniature scythes with razor-sharp edges

Christmas tree spins into action attacking wedding guests

Trees are operated by Santa Roboforms using remote control

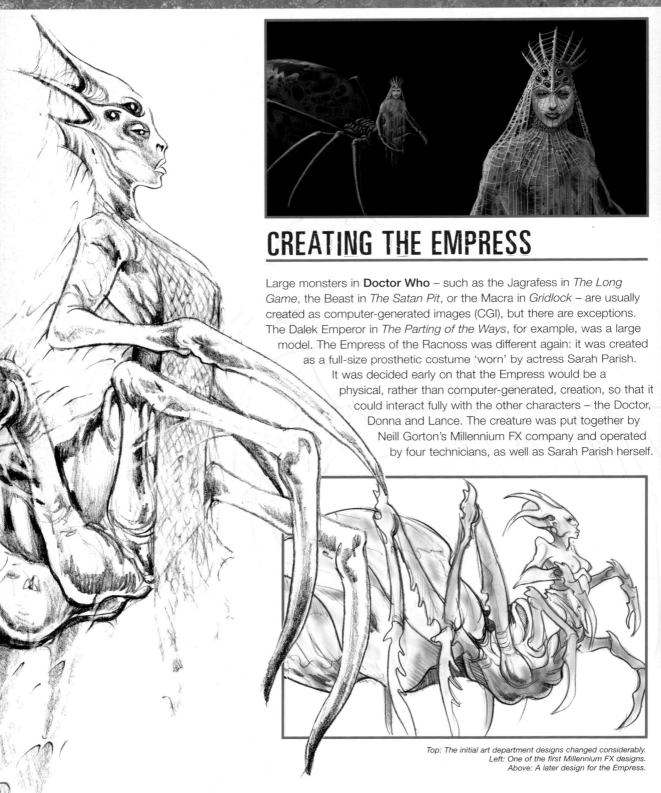

CREATING THE EMPRESS

Large monsters in **Doctor Who** – such as the Jagrafess in *The Long Game*, the Beast in *The Satan Pit*, or the Macra in *Gridlock* – are usually created as computer-generated images (CGI), but there are exceptions. The Dalek Emperor in *The Parting of the Ways*, for example, was a large model. The Empress of the Racnoss was different again: it was created as a full-size prosthetic costume 'worn' by actress Sarah Parish. It was decided early on that the Empress would be a physical, rather than computer-generated, creation, so that it could interact fully with the other characters – the Doctor, Donna and Lance. The creature was put together by Neill Gorton's Millennium FX company and operated by four technicians, as well as Sarah Parish herself.

Top: The initial art department designs changed considerably.
Left: One of the first Millennium FX designs.
Above: A later design for the Empress.

The final creature was very different from the original ideas supplied by the **Doctor Who** art department. Millennium FX made a large clay model of the Empress, and from this worked out how to build the full-size creature. Sections were modelled in clay, or sculpted in polystyrene, then finished in fibreglass. The final creature was so large it could not be completely assembled in the company's workshops – and the first time the entire creature was put together was on location ready for filming.

Top: The clay model of the complete Empress.
Above and right: A life-size sculpture of the head.

THE EMPRESS OF THE RACNOSS

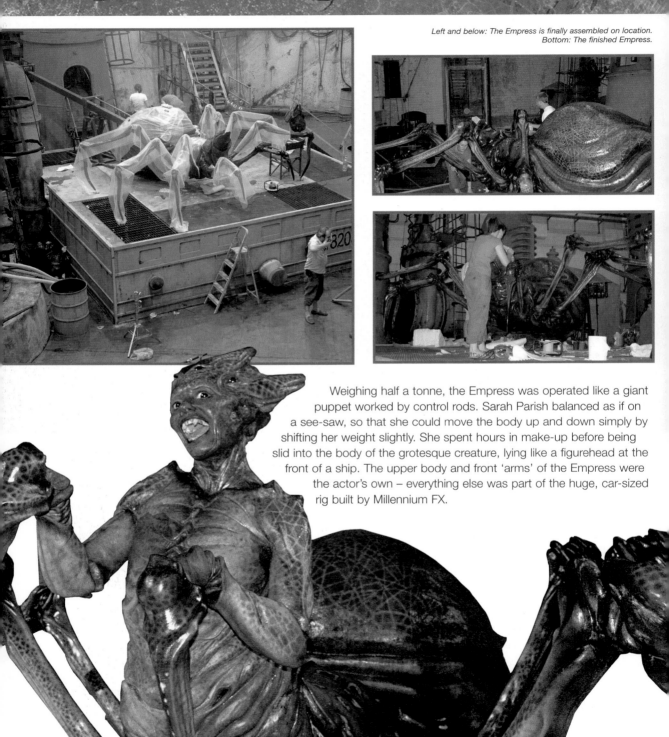

Left and below: The Empress is finally assembled on location.
Bottom: The finished Empress.

Weighing half a tonne, the Empress was operated like a giant puppet worked by control rods. Sarah Parish balanced as if on a see-saw, so that she could move the body up and down simply by shifting her weight slightly. She spent hours in make-up before being slid into the body of the grotesque creature, lying like a figurehead at the front of a ship. The upper body and front 'arms' of the Empress were the actor's own – everything else was part of the huge, car-sized rig built by Millennium FX.

FOLLOW THAT CAB!

One of the most impressive and exciting sequences in *The Runaway Bride* is where Donna is driven off in a taxi by a sinister Santa. Although set in London, only a small part of the chase was actually shot on the M4 – the rest was done on a link road in Cardiff. Many of the shots were achieved 'on the run' using a rolling roadblock – a cordon of police cars moving along the road while the **Doctor Who** production team worked in the cleared space between them.

The sequence took a huge amount of planning and preparation, and combined live-action stunt driving, computer-generated images (CGI – mainly of the TARDIS), and even live shots of David Tennant as the Doctor being hung over the road!

The pictures on this page show how the stunning, finished effect was planned and achieved.

Top and middle: Frames from The Mill showing where the TARDIS will be added to the shots.
Above: Shooting the TARDIS and the taxi.

THE GIANT MAGGOTS

The Giant Maggots are created when Global Chemicals dispose of waste from a revolutionary oil-refining process by pumping it down a disused coal mine. The green, chemical slime causes maggots in the mine to mutate, growing to an enormous size. And not only is the glowing, green waste deadly to anyone who touches it – so are the maggots.

The Doctor and his friends from UNIT try to destroy the creatures with armour-piercing bullets, flame-throwers and fire bombs before they discover the real solution – the Maggots can be poisoned with a type of fungus.

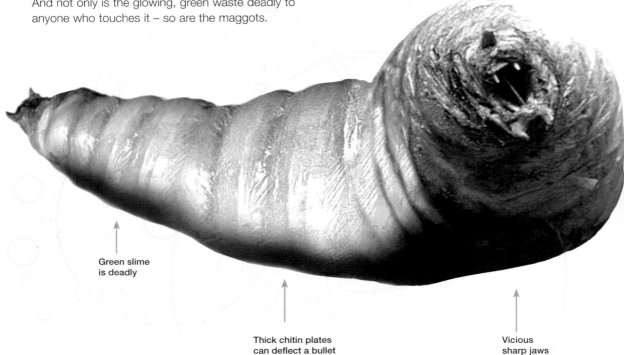

Green slime
is deadly

Thick chitin plates
can deflect a bullet

Vicious
sharp jaws

GLOBAL CHEMICALS AND BOSS

Global Chemicals is run by Justin Stevens, and its mission is to control the world through technological advancement. The company is actually controlled by a giant super-computer – BOSS – which is linked directly to Stevens' brain. It plans to take over humanity to ensure huge profits for Global Chemicals, but the Doctor manages to convince Stevens that BOSS must be destroyed.

THE GREEN DEATH

A mysterious death at a disused coal mine leads to a UNIT investigation. Teaming up with a local group of ecologists, the Doctor discovers that Global Chemicals has been dumping deadly chemical waste down the mine, and the waste has caused maggots to mutate and grow in size.

While the Brigadier and his men try to contain the maggots, the Doctor confronts the real head of Global Chemicals – a megalomaniac computer called BOSS that has the ability to take over people's minds and is planning world domination.

With BOSS ready to act, the race is on to stop the maggots before they metamorphose into something even more deadly.

Written by
Robert Sloman
Featuring
the Third Doctor,
UNIT and Jo
First broadcast
19 May 1973 –
23 June 1973
6 episodes

PROFESSOR CLIFF JONES

Nobel prizewinner Professor Cliff Jones is in charge of an ecological group based in the Welsh village of Llanfairfach. He is a champion of the use of solar power, the tides, wind and other renewable energy sources, rather than using up the Earth's resources.

A new, edible fungus his group is developing turns out to be deadly to the giant maggots and kills them. Cliff Jones asks the Doctor's assistant, Jo, if she will go with him on an expedition up the Amazon – as his wife. The Doctor's sadness is apparent when Jo agrees.

METEBELIS THREE

For a long time, the Doctor has wanted to visit Metebelis Three, the famous blue planet of the Acteon Galaxy. But when he gets there, it is not what he expected: as soon as he leaves the TARDIS, the Doctor is attacked by flying monsters.

He brings back one of the famous blue crystals, though, and uses its mind-opening properties to break the control of BOSS. He gives the crystal to Jo as a wedding present, little knowing that it is the last great perfect crystal of power and that the giant spiders of Metebelis Three will soon want it back.

GIANT FLY

As Professor Jones and his colleagues prepare to poison the maggots with their fungus, UNIT's Sergeant Benton finds a maggot that has entered a pupa stage. The maggots are about to change into something else.

Luckily only one of the maggots gets a chance to change before they are killed. It becomes a giant fly, attacking the Doctor from the air and squirting poisonous green fluid at him. The Doctor manages to swat it with his cape, and the beautiful but deadly creature is killed.

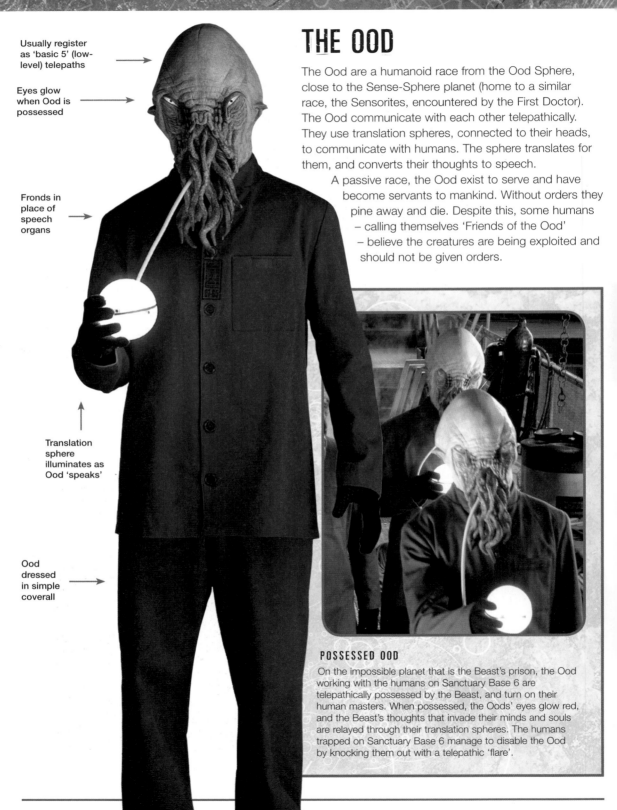

Usually register as 'basic 5' (low-level) telepaths

Eyes glow when Ood is possessed

Fronds in place of speech organs

Translation sphere illuminates as Ood 'speaks'

Ood dressed in simple coverall

THE OOD

The Ood are a humanoid race from the Ood Sphere, close to the Sense-Sphere planet (home to a similar race, the Sensorites, encountered by the First Doctor). The Ood communicate with each other telepathically. They use translation spheres, connected to their heads, to communicate with humans. The sphere translates for them, and converts their thoughts to speech.

A passive race, the Ood exist to serve and have become servants to mankind. Without orders they pine away and die. Despite this, some humans – calling themselves 'Friends of the Ood' – believe the creatures are being exploited and should not be given orders.

POSSESSED OOD

On the impossible planet that is the Beast's prison, the Ood working with the humans on Sanctuary Base 6 are telepathically possessed by the Beast, and turn on their human masters. When possessed, the Oods' eyes glow red, and the Beast's thoughts that invade their minds and souls are relayed through their translation spheres. The humans trapped on Sanctuary Base 6 manage to disable the Ood by knocking them out with a telepathic 'flare'.

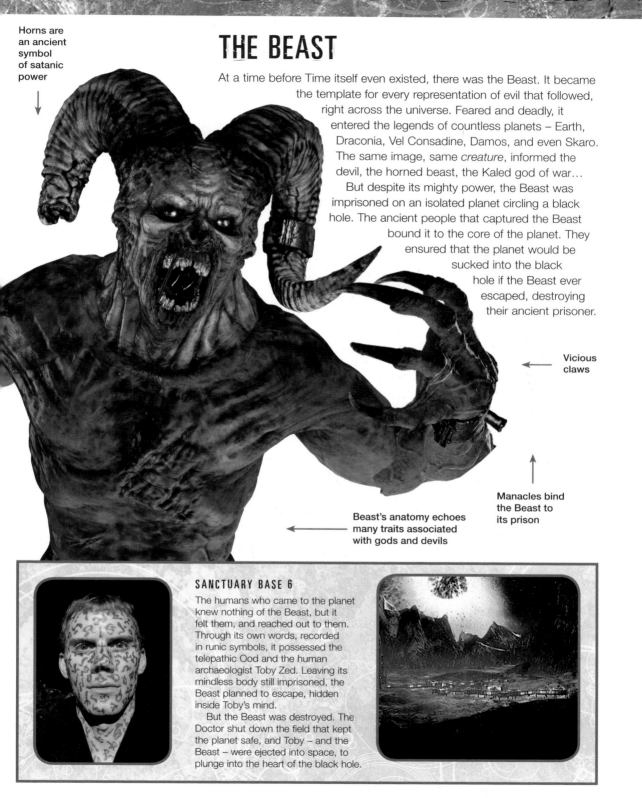

Horns are
an ancient
symbol
of satanic
power

THE BEAST

At a time before Time itself even existed, there was the Beast. It became
the template for every representation of evil that followed,
right across the universe. Feared and deadly, it
entered the legends of countless planets – Earth,
Draconia, Vel Consadine, Damos, and even Skaro.
The same image, same *creature*, informed the
devil, the horned beast, the Kaled god of war…
But despite its mighty power, the Beast was
imprisoned on an isolated planet circling a black
hole. The ancient people that captured the Beast
bound it to the core of the planet. They
ensured that the planet would be
sucked into the black
hole if the Beast ever
escaped, destroying
their ancient prisoner.

Vicious
claws

Manacles bind
the Beast to
its prison

Beast's anatomy echoes
many traits associated
with gods and devils

SANCTUARY BASE 6

The humans who came to the planet
knew nothing of the Beast, but it
felt them, and reached out to them.
Through its own words, recorded
in runic symbols, it possessed the
telepathic Ood and the human
archaeologist Toby Zed. Leaving its
mindless body still imprisoned, the
Beast planned to escape, hidden
inside Toby's mind.

But the Beast was destroyed. The
Doctor shut down the field that kept
the planet safe, and Toby – and the
Beast – were ejected into space, to
plunge into the heart of the black hole.

The Doctor and Ida Scott discover the Satan Pit.

THE IMPOSSIBLE PLANET and THE SATAN PIT

Written by
Matthew Jones
Featuring
the Tenth Doctor
and Rose
First broadcast
3 June 2006 –
10 June 2006
2 episodes

The Doctor and Rose arrive on Sanctuary Base 6, on a planet in an impossible orbit around a black hole. The crew and their servants, the Ood, are drilling to find the power source that keeps the planet safe – but the planet is the prison of the Beast, and they have awakened it.

The Beast turns the Ood against the humans, and also possesses archaeologist Toby Zed. It plans to escape from the planet inside Toby's mind (the only way it can leave without being sucked into the black hole).

The Doctor finds the Beast's animalistic body chained up inside the planet, and realises the truth. He plunges the planet into the black hole, and Rose ejects the possessed Toby into space.

KROP TOR

The planet that is prison to the Beast now has no name, but in the scriptures of the Veltino – an ancient race that, perhaps, knew of the Beast – it is called Krop Tor, which means 'the bitter pill'. A vestige of truth survived in their legends – they believed that the black hole was itself a demon who was tricked into devouring the planet, only to spit it out because it was poison.

Since the Beast was imprisoned, the planet has been in orbit around the black hole K-37 Gem 5. If the Beast escapes, the planet will be destroyed.

SANCTUARY CREW

Since the death of their captain, the principal members of the Sanctuary Base 6 crew are: Zachary Cross Flane (Acting Captain), Ida Scott (Science Officer), John Jefferson (Head of Security), Danny Bartock (Ethics Committee), Toby Zed (Archaeologist) and Scooti Manista (Trainee Maintenance). There is also a complement of 50 Ood.

The base was brought to the planet in sections that snap together, and established so that the crew can find the energy source that stops it from being pulled into the black hole.

ANCIENT RUNES

The words of the Beast appear as runic symbols on ancient artefacts discovered by Toby – so ancient that the TARDIS cannot translate them. The Beast also speaks through those it has possessed.

An Ood serves Rose her meal and tells her: 'The Beast and his armies shall rise from the Pit to make war against God.' Toby hears a disembodied voice before he is possessed, and runes are etched into his face and hands. As the Beast takes control of him, he tells his colleagues he understands the runes: 'These are the words of the Beast …'

BRINGING THE OOD TO LIFE

Originally, the Doctor's enemies the Slitheen were to be with the humans on Sanctuary Base 6, but as the script developed, it was felt that a new race of aliens would fit the story better. These episodes were the last to be made in the second season of **Doctor Who**, and it was up to Millennium FX to produce as many Ood as possible, as quickly as they could. The fact that the Ood have no visible mouths, are all identical, and wear simple coveralls, helped to keep costs down. Millennium FX made 12 Ood, though computer graphics made it seem that there were more. One of the masks had animatronics built in so that it could change expression. Millennium FX also provided the Ood translation spheres, which lit up when the actor pressed a switch on the back.

The Ood ended up being every bit as impressive and 'eerily elegant' as the script originally described them.

Left: The art department's initial concept for an Ood.
Top: The Ood on location.
Above: Fitting an Ood mask to an actor.

DOCTOR WHO II		TITLE	BEAST CAVERN
DRAWN BY:	PETER MCKINSTRY		DATE: 1.02.06
PRODUCER:	SUP ART DIRECTOR:		CONSTRUCTION:
DIRECTOR:	S/B ART DIRECTOR:		FABRICATION:
DOP:	SET DECORATOR:		GRAPHICS:
PROD DESIGNER:	PROPS MASTER:		COSTUME

© BBC CYMRU WALES 2005

This page shows some initial concept designs for the Satan Pit together with (left middle) the Doctor's meeting with the Beast as it appeared on screen.

CREATING THE BEAST

The Beast was created entirely as a computer-generated image (CGI) by effects house The Mill – there was no model, no costume and no actor, as such. Even more amazingly, it was devised in just six weeks by two of The Mill's animators, working from designs drawn up by Nicholas Hernandez. He, in turn, was working from an idea provided by a Mill employee who actually worked in the despatch department.

As with all computer-generated characters, the Beast was created from the final design drawings as a rough, wireframe model that could be animated. Then each frame of the Beast was given colour and texture until it looked just like a real – hellish – creature.

Though the Beast creature never actually speaks, its movements had to be matched exactly with footage of David Tennant playing the Doctor. As happens so often in the making of **Doctor Who**, David Tennant was acting against a green screen, which was replaced with The Mill's work.

THE ISOLUS

The Isolus are empathic beings of intense emotion, similar in appearance to cosmic flowers. They drift through space, with only each other for company.

The Isolus mother jettisons millions of fledgeling spores – children – who depend on each other for the empathic link that sustains them. Each child travels inside a pod, riding the heat and energy of solar tides. They take thousands of years to grow to adulthood, so to alleviate their boredom they play together.

Their games involve using their ionic power to create make-believe worlds where they can play, feeding off each other's love and kinship.

The Isolus child that takes over Chloe Webber has been cast adrift from its fellows by a solar flare. Desperate for friendship – for love – it continues trying to create make-believe worlds where it can play.

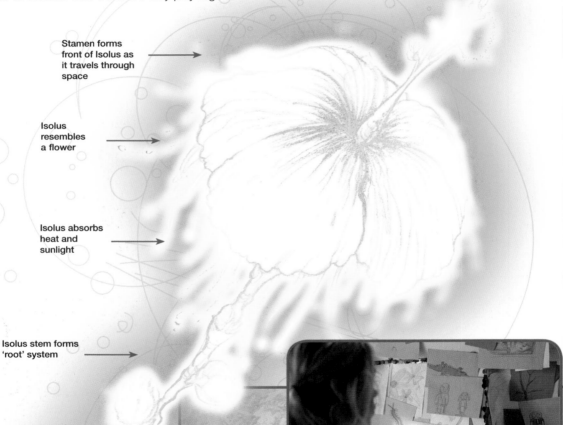

Stamen forms front of Isolus as it travels through space

Isolus resembles a flower

Isolus absorbs heat and sunlight

Isolus stem forms 'root' system

CHLOE WEBBER'S MOVING PICTURES

Desperate for friendship and company, the Isolus inside Chloe still tries to create its own worlds. It puts real people – the neighbourhood children – inside the pictures that Chloe draws. They capture the entire audience of the 2012 London Olympics opening ceremony inside a picture. But the Isolus is still lonely, so Chloe then starts to draw the entire world.

The Isolus can also bring Chloe's drawings to life using ionic energy. A crossed-out mistake becomes a ball of graphite scribble that attacks Rose. More frighteningly, a drawing of Chloe's violent father, who recently died, comes to life to threaten Chloe and her mother Trish.

FEAR HER

The people of Dame Kelly Holmes Close are preparing for the 2012 Olympics, but children are going missing. They are being trapped inside the drawings of 12-year-old Chloe Webber, who has been possessed by a lonely, lost Isolus child, separated from its mother and protective pod.

   With the Doctor imprisoned in a drawing, Rose tries to help Chloe and her mother before a picture of Chloe's unpleasant father is brought to life by the Isolus. The Olympic audience disappears from the stadium as Chloe draws it. Then – determined to provide enough friends for the Isolus – she begins a picture of the world. But Rose uses the heat of the Olympic flame to power the pod and reunite the creature with its family.

Written by
Matthew Graham
Featuring
the Tenth Doctor
and Rose
First broadcast
24 June 2006
1 episode

SCRIBBLE MONSTER

One of Chloe's discarded drawings comes to life as a scribble monster, which attacks Rose. The Doctor stops it with his sonic screwdriver. Back in the TARDIS, he realises it is an animated ball of graphite – made from the same material as the lead of an ordinary pencil. He is able to rub some of it out with an eraser.

   The creature has been animated by the same ionic energy the Isolus uses to capture people and imprison them inside Chloe's drawings.

CHLOE'S FATHER

Chloe Webber's father died a year ago. Both Chloe and her mother, Trish, were frightened of Mr Webber. To calm Chloe down, Trish would sing the 'Kookaburra' song to her ('Kookaburra sits in the old gum tree…').

   But Chloe has drawn a picture of her father, and hidden it inside her wardrobe. The ionic energy from the Isolus child brings the picture to life as Chloe's fear increases, and the drawing of her dad threatens to come after Chloe and Trish. It becomes a harmless drawing again after the Isolus leaves Earth.

THE ISOLUS POD

Each Isolus child travels inside a pod, which is powered by the heat of the stars. When one pod crashes in Dame Kelly Holmes Close, it absorbs heat from the area to convert into power. As a result, the close seems unseasonably cold. The new tarmac laid on the road blisters in the heat from the pod. The pod affects other energy sources, so that cars stop when they pass it.

   Rose uses the heat – and love – of the Olympic flame to power up the pod fully and send it back on its journey through the stars.

THE ISOLUS

WORD PICTURES

Writer Matthew Graham was originally asked to come up with a story for Series Three of **Doctor Who**, to be broadcast in 2007, but as things turned out, his script was moved forward to become one of the later episodes of the 2006 series. An experienced television scriptwriter, Matthew is best known as the co-creator and lead writer of the BBC series **Life on Mars**. There is a strange connection between the two series. When Matthew asked his daughter, Daisy, to come up with a surname for the **Life on Mars** hero Sam, she chose Tyler. It was only later – once Sam Tyler was named – that Daisy told her father she'd suggested the name because the Doctor's companion was Rose Tyler.

Matthew was originally asked to come up with a story that was set in a limited location – such as a bunker. This proved rather restrictive, and instead he brought the Doctor and Rose down to Earth, literally, by wondering what would happen if they turned up in an ordinary city street.

But right from the start, the story was always going to be about drawings that somehow came to life. Matthew explains: 'I suggested demonic or possessed children's drawings, pictures where people's eyes follow you round the room. Children's drawings always have big eyes and big hair and stick arms, so what if they move?'

CHARACTER SKETCHES

Chloe's drawings were actually created by 12-year-old Indigo Rumbelow, under the guidance of **Doctor Who** storyboard artist Shaun Williams. For sequences where Chloe had to be seen to be drawing, actor Abisola Agbaje was given versions sketched out in faint pencil, which she could simply draw over, so it looked as though Chloe was drawing the pictures from scratch.

CREATING THE ISOLUS CHILD

The Isolus child itself also started life as a drawing. Initial concept sketches produced by the **Doctor Who** art department were fleshed out into the final, flower-like design and created as animated computer images by effects house The Mill.

Above: Design drawings for the Isolus child.
Below: The computer-generated creature finds Chloe.

SCRIPT EXTRACT

```
Bright sunlight. CHLOE (ordinary, happy kid)
looks up from her desk.
FX: A single white Isolus flower floats into her
room.

CHLOE (Voice Over)
My pod was drawn to heat. I was drawn to Chloe
Webber.

CHLOE stands as -
FX: the Isolus child drifts closer.

CHLOE (continued)
She was like me. Alone. She needed me and I her.

FX: The flower flies into CHLOE's mouth. She
literally inhales it. Looks stunned. Faints on
the spot.
```

THE JUDOON

The Judoon are a police force available for hire. Other races employ them to carry out inter-planetary law-enforcement tasks on their behalf. Arriving in massive vertical spaceships, which resemble huge tower blocks, they can only enforce galactic law when specifically invited to do so, or on neutral territory.

Ruthless in the extreme, the Judoon have little interest in other life forms apart from whether they obey the letter of the law. Anyone who opposes them is automatically found guilty of assault and executed.

Strong keratin horns

Heavy, effective armour covers tough hide of Judoon

Heavy, armoured battle gauntlets

Scanning device

Translator

INTERROGATION

When searching for the Plasmavore, the Judoon use highly advanced scanning technology to check that the people at Royal Hope Hospital are human. The scanner emits a blue light and the Judoon take a reading from the device.

Once someone is proved to be human, the Judoon use the other end of the same device to mark them on the back of the hand with an X. The ink used is fused with a distinctive compound so it cannot be forged.

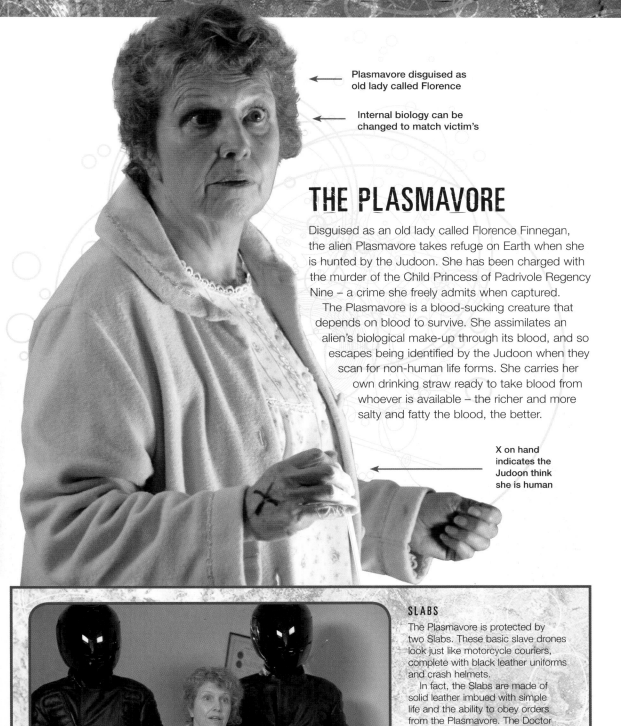

Plasmavore disguised as old lady called Florence

Internal biology can be changed to match victim's

THE PLASMAVORE

Disguised as an old lady called Florence Finnegan, the alien Plasmavore takes refuge on Earth when she is hunted by the Judoon. She has been charged with the murder of the Child Princess of Padrivole Regency Nine – a crime she freely admits when captured.

The Plasmavore is a blood-sucking creature that depends on blood to survive. She assimilates an alien's biological make-up through its blood, and so escapes being identified by the Judoon when they scan for non-human life forms. She carries her own drinking straw ready to take blood from whoever is available – the richer and more salty and fatty the blood, the better.

X on hand indicates the Judoon think she is human

SLABS

The Plasmavore is protected by two Slabs. These basic slave drones look just like motorcycle couriers, complete with black leather uniforms and crash helmets.

In fact, the Slabs are made of solid leather imbued with simple life and the ability to obey orders from the Plasmavore. The Doctor manages to destroy one of the Slabs, while the Judoon easily deal with the other one.

MARTHA JONES

Training to become a doctor at the Royal Hope Hospital in London, Martha Jones is more than a little surprised when the whole hospital is transported to the moon.

The Doctor is immediately impressed with Martha's calm analysis of the situation – and her enthusiasm and awe at their new surroundings. She can see the beauty of the lunar landscape as well as appreciate the danger they are in. He trusts her to revive him after he allows the Plasmavore to drink his blood, and to understand what he has done and make sure the Judoon bring the creature to justice.

After returning safely to Earth, the Doctor offers Martha 'just one trip' in the TARDIS, but they become such good friends that this soon becomes two trips, and then many, many more.

SMITH AND JONES

The Judoon are hunting for a Plasmavore, and have tracked her to the Royal Hope Hospital in London. They use an H_2O scoop to transport the hospital to the neutral territory of the moon, and then hunt for any non-human life forms. The Doctor and his new friend Martha try to evade the Judoon – who will assume the Doctor is their prey if they find him – and unmask the real Plasmavore, disguised as an old lady called Florence.

Cornered, the Plasmavore tries to use the MRI scanner to destroy all other life in the hospital – and on half of the Earth. But having absorbed the Doctor's blood, she registers as non-human and is executed. Safely back on Earth, the Doctor offers Martha a trip in the TARDIS.

Written by
Russell T Davies
Featuring
the Tenth Doctor
and Martha
First broadcast
31 March 2007
1 episode

H_2O SCOOP

The Judoon have access to a range of technology, including universal galactic real-time translation systems, so they can communicate with other life forms – such as humans.

They sometimes use an H_2O scoop, harnessing the inert power of hydrogen, to transport people or entire buildings to neutral space where the Judoon can enforce the law. When the scoop is used it creates what looks like a powerful lightning and thunder storm – but with the rain going up from the ground to the gathering clouds above.

MAGNETIC PULSE

The Plasmavore plans to destroy the Judoon using the Royal Hope Hospital's Magnetic Resonance Imaging scanner. She adapts it to emit a force of 50,000 tesla, enough to fry the brainstem of any living creature within 50,000 miles … including the side of the Earth facing the moon. The Plasmavore will herself be screened from the emission and safe.

Luckily, the Doctor is able to turn the machine off after the Plasmavore is executed.

MARTHA'S FAMILY

Martha has an older sister, Tish, and a younger brother called Leo. Leo has a girlfriend called Shonara and a daughter, Keisha. Martha's mother and father are Francine and Clive, and they have separated. Francine does not approve of Clive's new – much younger – girlfriend Annalise. This makes Leo's twenty-first-birthday party rather fraught.

After the party, Martha meets the Doctor again, and accepts his offer of a trip in the TARDIS – which she is astonished to find is much bigger inside than outside!

MOON LANDINGS

The effects of transporting the Royal Hope Hospital to the moon, and the empty crater it leaves behind in London, were achieved by The Mill using computer-generated images (CGI). The massive Judoon spaceships were also designed and created by The Mill.

The picture above shows the final image of the Judoon marching from their ships across the lunar landscape to the Royal Hope Hospital and passing through the protective shield that keeps the atmosphere in. Below is an early concept painting showing how the hospital might have looked when transported to the moon.

MAKING MONSTERS

While the Plasmavore is disguised as an old lady, and her deadly Slabs look like motorcycle messengers, the Judoon are obviously an alien race – this is conspicuous even when they are wearing their distinctively shaped helmets. And when the Judoon captain removes his helmet, the alien head beneath is revealed.

The impressive animatronic head was designed and created by Neill Gorton's team at Millennium FX. As the captain is the only Judoon to remove his helmet, just one head was needed, and this could be made as impressive as possible.

Top: Sculpting a full-size statue of the Judoon.
Above: Design paintings of the Judoon.
Right: The complicated animatronics housed inside the Judoon head.

THE KRYNOID

The Krynoid is a form of intelligent plant life that feeds on animals. On planets where the Krynoid takes hold, animal life becomes extinct. It can infect an animal with its spores, causing the 'host' creature to mutate into a Krynoid, which retains some of that host's knowledge, memory and intelligence. The Krynoid is also able to transfer some of its power to the local vegetation, making plant life hostile and deadly.

No one knows for sure how Krynoid plant pods travel through space. One theory is that their planet of origin is volcanic, and the pods are shot out (in pairs) by the eruptions.

Tentacles like branches and roots

Krynoid does not need nitrogen to survive

Krynoid grows from large gourd-like plant

Krynoid is mobile and seeks out food

TRANSITION STAGES

The first person to be infected with the Krynoid is Charles Winlett, one of the team that discovers the Krynoid pods. The scientists put one of the pods under ultraviolet light and, when it opens, a shoot emerges, which attacks Winlett. Winlett's body is taken over by the Krynoid. His temperature and heart rate drop drastically and his skin becomes green and blotchy. The Doctor discovers that Winlett's blood is infected with plant bacteria and soon his whole body begins to change into a Krynoid.

The fully developed Krynoid attacks Chase's mansion.

THE SEEDS OF DOOM

A mysterious alien plant pod is discovered in Antarctica – a Krynoid. It infects one of the team who found it and he mutates. But the millionaire plant-collector Harrison Chase has heard about the Krynoid and is determined to own it. The Krynoid is destroyed, but the Doctor discovers a second pod, which is stolen by Chase's men.

The Doctor and Sarah follow Chase to his country house and find that one of his team has already been infected and is mutating. With the creature now able to control all plant life, and about to germinate and send out millions of pods, the Doctor has no choice but to ask UNIT to send in the RAF to bomb the house and destroy the Krynoid.

Written by
Robert Banks Stewart
Featuring
the Fourth Doctor
and Sarah
First broadcast
31 January 1976 –
6 March 1976
6 episodes

HARRISON CHASE

Desperate to acquire the Krynoid for his extensive collection of plants, Harrison Chase sends his unscrupulous hitman Scorby to Antarctica to steal the pod.

Once he has a Krynoid, Chase sets out to cultivate it, allowing it to infect one of his scientists – Keeler. Chase is sympathetic to the aims of the Krynoid, feeling humans have neglected the most beautiful parts of nature. He is taken over by the Krynoid as it grows to a giant size, and traps the Doctor and Sarah inside his house. He is finally killed in his own compost machine.

THE ANTARCTIC BASE

The first Krynoid pod is discovered by scientists based in an Antarctic camp run by the World Ecology Bureau. Chase's henchmen arrive in a plane, pretending they are lost, then take the crew hostage and demand the pod. Despite the Doctor's best efforts, they get the second pod and escape, sabotaging the base's power plant so it explodes.

The Doctor and Sarah escape, rescued by a Royal Marine survival team sent in to help. But scientists Stevenson and Moberley have already been killed by the mutating Winlett.

WORLD ECOLOGY BUREAU

Sir Colin Thackeray is in charge of the World Ecology Bureau, which is based in London. His deputy, a disgruntled man called Dunbar, has told Harrison Chase about the discovery of the Krynoid pod in exchange for money. Though Dunbar later sees the error of his ways, the damage has been done and Chase gets hold of a Krynoid – which later kills Dunbar as he tries to make amends.

Sir Colin Thackeray has heard of the Doctor through his association with UNIT, and later calls in UNIT to help destroy the Krynoid.

THE LAND OF FICTION

When the Doctor is forced to use the TARDIS's Emergency Unit to escape from a volcanic eruption on the planet Dulkis (see page 82), the TARDIS arrives first in a white void and then in what seems to be a forest. The Doctor discovers that the trees are all in the shape of letters – with lines of trees spelling out sayings and proverbs – and he realises they are in a place where anything is possible: the Land of Fiction.

The Land of Fiction exists outside the normal space–time dimension and is ruled by the Master of Fiction, who lives in a citadel on top of a massive cliff.

On their way to the citadel, the Doctor and his companions, Jamie and Zoe, meet many fictional characters from novels, fairy tales and mythology – all existing as if they were real in this strange world.

TOY SOLDIERS

While the White Robots seem to patrol the empty void and the Master of Fiction's citadel, his servants in the forest and the Land of Fiction are soldiers. But, as they soon discover, the soldiers who pursue the Doctor and his companions are actually life-size clockwork toys with huge keys in their backs.

They make a noise like grating cogwheels as they walk and can 'see' through a light in their hat. These images are linked to the Master of Fiction's scanner, so that he can watch what the soldiers do.

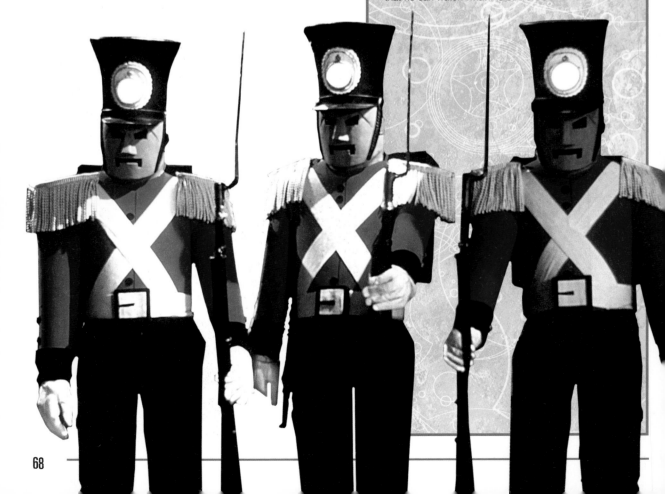

Rapunzel lets down her hair for Jamie.

THE MIND ROBBER

Arriving in the Land of Fiction, the Doctor, Jamie and Zoe meet Gulliver, who tells them of the Master of Fiction who rules the Land. Narrowly avoiding an attack by a unicorn, as well as encounters with Medusa and the Minotaur, they make their way to the citadel. On the way, the Doctor must solve riddles to rescue a trapped Zoe, and do a jigsaw puzzle to replace Jamie's face – when he gets it wrong, Jamie's face changes.

Finally the Doctor meets the Master of Fiction and the computer he serves, which wants the Doctor to replace the frail Master of Fiction and help it take over the Earth. But the Doctor enlists the help of fictional heroes against the Master of Fiction, and the computer is destroyed.

Written by
Peter Ling
Featuring
the Second Doctor,
Jamie and Zoe
First broadcast
14 September 1968 –
12 October 1968
5 episodes

EMERGENCY UNIT

The Emergency Unit shifts the TARDIS out of the space–time dimension – out of reality. It arrives 'nowhere': none of its meters and dials register anything and the scanner is blank.

Despite the Doctor's warning, both Zoe and Jamie venture outside into the void (tempted by images of their homes) and are menaced by White Robots. The Doctor manages to get his companions back, but then the TARDIS explodes and they are stranded in a strange forest.

WHITE ROBOTS

The White Robots that close in on Jamie and Zoe in the void outside the TARDIS serve the Master of Fiction. Perhaps the robots were created by the same power that made the computer, or perhaps they are also fictional creations that have been made real.

The robot costumes were first used in another science-fiction television series (pictured below) – so they are fictional!

THE MASTER OF FICTION

The Master of Fiction is actually an elderly human writer who was taken from his desk by the Master Brain when he dozed off on a hot summer's day in 1926. He created 'The Adventures of Captain Jack Harkaway' for *The Ensign*, a boys' magazine, and wrote 5000 words every week for 25 years – which is why he was selected for the post in the Land of Fiction.

His imagination and creativity give life to the inhabitants of the Land, so he cannot leave, but he is nearing death, and the Doctor is an ideal candidate for his replacement.

The Master of Fiction is actually controlled by the 'Master Brain' – a computer that feeds off the Master of Fiction's thoughts – but once the Doctor's mind is linked to the computer, he can foil its plan to take over the Earth and enslave its people, by calling up fictional heroes to help his cause.

FICTIONAL CHARACTERS

During their time in the Land of Fiction, the Doctor and his friends meet many characters from stories – myths, fairy tales, novels and even the hourly telepress of Zoe's time.

Rapunzel lets down her long hair to enable Jamie to climb into the Master of Fiction's citadel, while the Doctor meets a group of school children. All the time-travellers are charged by a unicorn, and the Doctor and Zoe face the snake-haired Medusa, who could turn them to stone if they look at her – as well as the Minotaur.

The most helpful of the characters they meet is Lemuel Gulliver, who can only speak the words written for him by his author: Dean Jonathan Swift. He tells the Doctor that he set sail from Bristol on 4 May 1699, and provides directions to the citadel.

One character that the Doctor does not recognise, but Zoe does, is the Karkus – a superhero who features in the hourly telepress of her time. He carries an anti-molecular ray disintegrator (which disappears when the Doctor points out that the weapon is scientifically impossible).

In a final battle between the Master of Fiction and the Doctor, the Master of Fiction summons the swordsman Cyrano de Bergerac (who is apparently angered that Jamie and Zoe poked fun at his enormous nose). To combat him, the Doctor conjures up D'Artagnan from the novel *The Three Musketeers*. When the Master of Fiction 'cancels' Cyrano de Bergerac and substitutes the pirate Blackbeard, the Doctor changes D'Artagnan to Sir Lancelot – in full armour.

The Doctor encounters Cyrano de Bergerac and D'Artagnan (top), Rapunzel (above) and the Medusa (right).

Known as the scourge of the galaxy M87, the Macra are massive crustaceans that depend on gas for their existence, consuming it like food. At one time, they enslaved human colonists, brainwashing them to believe that the gas was valuable. The colonists then, unwittingly, mined the gas for the Macra, who secretly controlled and regulated the humans' lives.

By the time of the human colonisation of New Earth in the far future, the Macra have devolved into less intelligent, more instinctive creatures, which hunt in a herd. The Doctor encounters them when he is trying to rescue Martha from a traffic jam below the city.

The Macra escaped from New New York Zoo when power was lost and the facility broke down. They made their way to the Undercity, where they found the gas they need to survive. The Macra attack the cars that stray too close purely on instinct and to preserve their territory, as a human might swat at a fly.

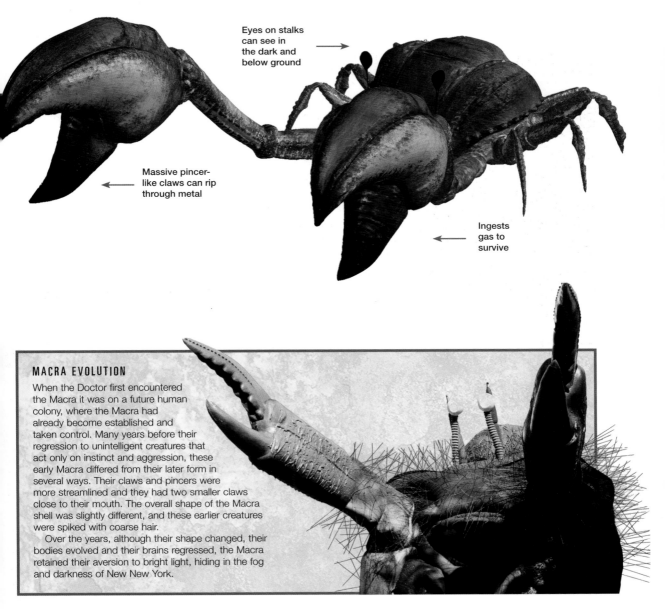

Eyes on stalks can see in the dark and below ground

Massive pincer-like claws can rip through metal

Ingests gas to survive

MACRA EVOLUTION

When the Doctor first encountered the Macra it was on a future human colony, where the Macra had already become established and taken control. Many years before their regression to unintelligent creatures that act only on instinct and aggression, these early Macra differed from their later form in several ways. Their claws and pincers were more streamlined and they had two smaller claws close to their mouth. The overall shape of the Macra shell was slightly different, and these earlier creatures were spiked with coarse hair.

Over the years, although their shape changed, their bodies evolved and their brains regressed, the Macra retained their aversion to bright light, hiding in the fog and darkness of New New York.

The real power behind the colony is revealed: the Macra.

THE MACRA TERROR

Written by
Ian Stuart Black
Featuring
the Second Doctor,
Ben, Polly and Jamie
First broadcast
11 March 1967 –
1 April 1967
4 episodes

The Doctor and his friends arrive on an apparently idyllic colony world. But after being welcomed warmly by the colonists, a voice speaks to the travellers as they sleep, brainwashing them.

The whole colony is actually controlled by the Macra, who have conditioned the colonists to mine the gas they need to survive. Jamie is sent down the mines – and becomes the first person ever to escape. Ben, meanwhile, is entirely under the influence of the Macra, and even betrays his friends, until the Doctor is able to break his conditioning.

The Doctor manages to expose the truth to the colonists, and the Macra are defeated when the Doctor destroys the gas pumps.

THE COLONY

The unnamed colony seems idyllic, but underneath this exterior lurks a terrible secret. The 'Controller' is in fact a frail old man, enslaved and controlled himself by the hideous Macra. The colonists have been brainwashed to serve the Macra and mine the gas they need. Anyone who throws off this conditioning, or who is foolish enough to wander out into the colony at night, is killed or taken for 'correction' at the hospital.

Once released from the Macra's mind control, the colonists realise how they have been manipulated.

THE GAS

The Macra have subverted the colony so that it now exists to produce gas for them to survive. The colonists have been brainwashed to believe that they depend on the gas themselves, and work constantly to mine and refine it.

The colony is located over rock that is rich in a type of salt that generates the gases the Macra need. These same gases are poisonous to the human colonists, however, and they cannot survive for long in the mines without special goggles and breathing masks.

THE PILOT

In charge of the day-to-day running of the colony, the Pilot is one of the few people who knows the formula of the gas the Macra need. Like everyone else in the colony, he is under the influence of the Macra, and is constantly quoting feel-good phrases such as: Hard work never hurt anybody … Nothing succeeds like success … If at first you don't succeed, try, try again …

Despite his conditioning, the Pilot's inclination is to be fair and uphold justice in the colony, even before the Doctor shows him the truth about the Macra.

GRIDLOCK

The Doctor takes his new friend Martha Jones to New Earth in the year five billion and fifty-three, to show her the far-distant future of humanity. But they arrive in the Undercity, where the citizens struggle to survive in harsh conditions and use patches to heighten their emotions. The whole airborne traffic system is almost at a standstill and Martha is kidnapped by motorists so they can move into the faster 'car share' lane.

But something is stirring in the depths of the Undercity: giant Macra are attacking the cars and dragging away motorists. The Doctor struggles to rescue Martha, but finds himself taken by Novice Hame to meet the Face of Boe, who has a final message to deliver…

Written by
Russell T Davies
Featuring
the Tenth Doctor
and Martha
First broadcast
14 April 2007
1 episode

NEW NEW YORK

By the time the Doctor and Martha visit New New York, it is a dying city. The ruling Senate has died – killed by a mutated version of a drug called 'Bliss'. Now the whole city is at a standstill, with traffic gridlocked and taking years to travel just a few miles.

Without power, the Undercity would long since have fallen into the sea, and the Doctor is able to use the last reserves to open the roof of the motorway tunnel. The trapped motorists are able to escape the gridlock to repopulate and revitalise the dying city.

THE FACE OF BOE

When the Senate was killed and the city of New New York started to die, it was the Face of Boe who saved it. He sacrificed himself for the city by wiring himself into the city mainframe to keep it running using his own life force.

But the Face is dying from the effort, and is desperate to speak to the Doctor. There is a legend that, when the Face of Boe dies, the sky will crack asunder – which it does for the motorists when the Doctor opens the tunnel roof. It is also said that he will speak one last secret, to a homeless, wandering traveller.

NOVICE HAME

Once one of the Sisters of Plenitude that ran the huge medical facility outside New New York, Novice Hame now acts as nurse to the dying Face of Boe. She regards this as her penance for past sins, and stays with the Face through the years that he keeps the city alive.

When the mutated virus killed the Senators, the Face of Boe kept Novice Hame safe by shrouding her in protective smoke. He sends her to rescue the Doctor from the gridlock, knowing the Doctor is the only person who can save the city as the Face dies.

BUILDING NEW NEW YORK

As well as the terrifying Macra, digital-effects house The Mill also had to create the images of the New New York skyline. They had already provided views of New New York for the previous year's episode, *New Earth*, and built on this work to create new vistas and backgrounds. Some of the original footage from *New Earth* was reused, playing as scanner images when the Doctor and Martha arrive in the Undercity.

The Mill also created the massive traffic jam of air cars on the New New York underground motorway, and added live-action characters, such as the Doctor, to these digital images.

A further challenge was the creation of the vast Senate Chamber, complete with rotting skeletons for the dead senators. Again, these digital images had to be blended with live-action sequences, featuring the Doctor, Martha, Novice Hame and the Face of Boe.

SCRIPT EXTRACT

FX: the fog clears – though never disappearing – revealing, a good distance below, HUGE, SLOW, LUMBERING 60-FOOT CRABS. Massive crustaceans, a bed of them, piled on top of each other, with small, bright white shining eyes on stalks.

The topmost creatures slowly wave huge 20-foot front claws (not able to reach the level of the Businessman's Car). The claws snap lazily, with that terrible sound.

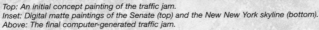
Top: An initial concept painting of the traffic jam.
Inset: Digital matte paintings of the Senate (top) and the New New York skyline (bottom).
Above: The final computer-generated traffic jam.

EFFECTS EVOLUTION

In the 1960s, visual effects on television were achieved very differently from today. Though many of the same physical effects techniques were used, in some form or another, the whole area of computer graphics did not exist. The first personal computer was not available until over a decade after *The Macra Terror* was made, and the only animation available was, in effect, cartoon drawings. This was obviously not an option for **Doctor Who**, and so the original Macra were built as real, very large, solid props. (Or, rather – because of the expense – just one prop! The effect of there being many Macra was achieved through clever editing.) The Macra prop was so big and unwieldy that it was fitted to the back of a van, so it could be moved round the studio. Its claws and appendages were operated by an actor inside the Macra.

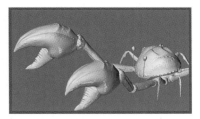

By the time *Gridlock* was made, digital-effects house The Mill had already proved how effective a totally computer-generated creature could be. The Beast from *The Satan Pit* (see page 51) was achieved entirely through computer-generated imagery (CGI), and The Mill rose magnificently to the challenge of creating a horde of giant crab monsters to threaten the Doctor and his friends once more.

Top: A series of pictures showing the rendering of the Macra, from wire-frame model to solid image, and the final textured creature.
Above: A car is about to feel the pinch.

A silicon life form from the planet Ogros, in Tau Ceti, the Ogri are sentient rocks. They feed on the amino acids and proteins that exist in the swamps on Ogros, the nearest equivalent on Earth being blood.

Brought to Earth by the villainous Cessair of Diplos, several Ogri have become part of the mysterious stone circle called the Nine Travellers, which explains why there are now more than nine stones in all. The Ogri have been active for a while – crushing the unfortunate Doctor Borlaise, who surveyed the stones in 1754.

Cessair keeps the Ogri fed with blood from ritual sacrifices of animals – and humans. As well as absorbing blood poured onto them, the Ogri suck the blood out of anyone who touches them, including two unfortunate campers. The Doctor believes that the Ogri have entered into Earth mythology, with the giants Gog and Magog, and the term 'ogre' all deriving from their name.

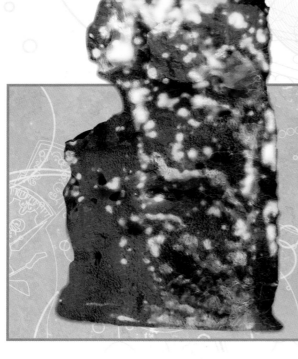

Ogri is made of heavy stone

Mistaken for part of stone circle, the Nine Travellers

Blood can be absorbed through surface

THE MEGARA

The two Megara who put the Doctor – and later Cessair – on trial appear as flashing, swirling lights. They are justice machines, but with living cells at their core, and act as combined judge, jury and – if necessary – executioner. Although the Doctor is acting in their interests, by releasing them to complete their duties, the Megara are literally-minded and put him on trial for this misdemeanour.

Being telepathic, the Megara can assess the level of truth in a witness's statement, but are not permitted to read memories to obtain evidence unless the witness is incapable through loss of consciousness, death, or natural stupidity.

The Doctor meets the Nine Travellers.

THE STONES OF BLOOD

The Doctor, Romana and K-9 have been sent to find the six segments of the Key to Time for the White Guardian. Tracking the third segment to Earth, they meet Professor Rumford, who is studying a strange stone circle. Several of the stones are actually alien Ogri, being fed on blood by a cult that worships a goddess known as the Calleach. The Doctor discovers that the Calleach is, in fact, the alien Cessair of Diplos.

When Romana is taken to a prison ship in hyperspace, the Doctor follows and releases the Megara to try Cessair for her crimes. The Doctor is put on trial, but convinces the Megara that Cessair is guilty. He retrieves the Great Seal of Diplos – the third segment of the Key to Time.

Written by
David Fisher
Featuring
the Fourth Doctor,
Romana and K-9
First broadcast
28 October 1978 –
18 November 1978
4 episodes

PROFESSOR RUMFORD

Professor Emilia Rumford is an expert on Bronze Age sites and is surveying the Nine Travellers. Stubborn and determined, she is initially sceptical of the Doctor and Romana's theories and suggestions. Only after she has been chased by one of the Ogri and found hidden portraits of the various aliases of Cessair of Diplos, does Professor Rumford begin to believe them.

When the Doctor follows Romana into hyperspace, he trusts Professor Rumford and K-9 to operate the equipment that can bring them both back.

CESSAIR OF DIPLOS

Charged with both murder and the theft of the Great Seal of Diplos, Cessair was kept on a prison ship in hyperspace, to be taken back to Diplos for trial by the Megara justice machines.

But Cessair escaped to Earth and assumed a number of identities over the 4000 years she lived there. Before masquerading as Vivien Fay, Cessair had previously been Mother Superior of the Little Sisters of St Gudula, the reclusive Mrs Tefusis, the Brazilian widow Senora Camara, and the 'wicked Lady Morgana Montcalm', who is said to have murdered her husband on their wedding night.

Tried and found guilty by the Megara following the Doctor's intervention, Cessair was sentenced to perpetual imprisonment – becoming one of the stones in the Nine Travellers. The Ogri she had taken were returned home.

GOING IN CIRCLES

As a location for *The Stones of Blood*, the **Doctor Who** production team used a real stone circle – the Rollright Stones, near Chipping Norton in the Cotswolds. Although steeped in legends and myths of its own, the stone circle was not quite what was needed: to become the Nine Travellers, a fake 'altar' stone, as well as two uprights with a plinth, were added, along with the Ogri stones themselves.

There were also several versions of the Nine Travellers. Some scenes – involving the Doctor's near-sacrifice, and the Calleach, for example – were shot in the studios at BBC Television Centre, on a specially constructed replica of the circle. Because the location material was shot on videotape rather than film (which was usually used for location filming), the match between the two is perfect and it's difficult to tell which is which.

An added complication was that, while the Nine Travellers are in the middle of deserted moorland, there is a road running past the Rollright Stones. So visual effects designer Mat Irvine made a model that was used for long shots of the entire circle.

Top: The model of the stone circle.
Middle: An Ogri arrives at the De Vries house.
Above: On location – an Ogri goes over the edge of a cliff.

THE OGRONS

The Ogrons are monstrous, ape-like creatures that live in scattered communities on a barren outer planet in the remote fringes of the galaxy. They worship and fear a large, shapeless monster that also lives on the planet. Because of their great strength, mindless obedience and inherent stupidity, the Ogrons are used as mercenaries by various other life forms.

Most notably, the Daleks used Ogrons as security troops to keep the human population of Earth under control after their invasion in the twenty-second century. (The full extent of their use of the Ogrons is still unknown.) The Daleks also allowed the Master to use the Ogrons to try to provoke a war between Earth and the Draconian Empire in the twenty-sixth century.

Top of head is a weak point

Ogrons will eat anything

Blaster pistol can stun or kill

Monstrous, ape-like appearance

ALIENS FOR HIRE

The Ogrons have been used as mercenaries for centuries by the Daleks. The Daleks rule them through fear, and use the Ogrons for security tasks and menial work that require little or no intelligence. After their invasion of Earth, the Daleks used human traitors in positions that required more intelligence, but the Ogrons answered directly to the Daleks.

The Master, a renegade Time Lord and the Doctor's sworn enemy, also used the Ogrons – possibly at the insistence of the Daleks, as he was himself working for them. Certainly, the Master finds it frustrating working with such stupid creatures, but he does not suffer fools gladly and planned all along to betray the Daleks when he could, himself, take control of the galaxy.

THE DRACONIANS

Reptilian humanoids, the Draconians had an empire that rivalled and bordered that of Earth. After a terrible war in the twenty-sixth century, there was an uneasy truce between the humans and the Draconians – or 'dragons' as the Earth forces nicknamed them.

The Draconians are ruled by a hereditary emperor, and are a race steeped in honour and tradition. They do not lie, and females are not permitted to speak in the presence of their 'betters', such as the emperor.

There is a legend of a man who came to Draconia during the time of the fifteenth Emperor and saved the Draconians from a great plague that threatened to wipe them out. He came in a strange ship called the TARDIS, and his name was the Doctor.

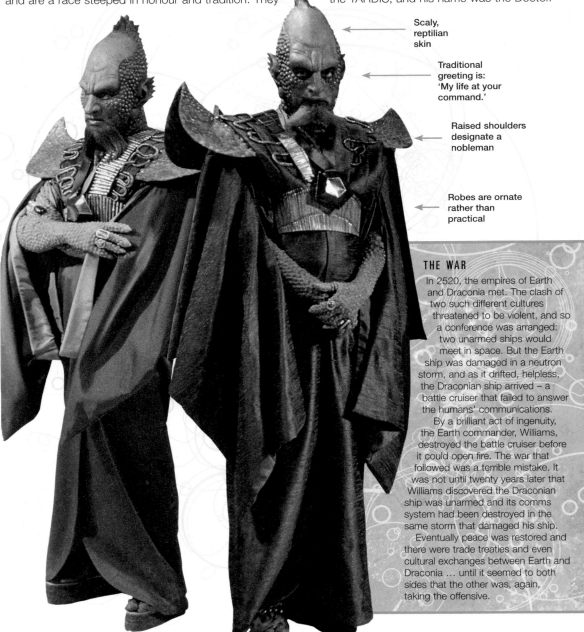

Scaly, reptilian skin

Traditional greeting is: 'My life at your command.'

Raised shoulders designate a nobleman

Robes are ornate rather than practical

THE WAR

In 2520, the empires of Earth and Draconia met. The clash of two such different cultures threatened to be violent, and so a conference was arranged: two unarmed ships would meet in space. But the Earth ship was damaged in a neutron storm, and as it drifted, helpless, the Draconian ship arrived – a battle cruiser that failed to answer the humans' communications.

By a brilliant act of ingenuity, the Earth commander, Williams, destroyed the battle cruiser before it could open fire. The war that followed was a terrible mistake. It was not until twenty years later that Williams discovered the Draconian ship was unarmed and its comms system had been destroyed in the same storm that damaged his ship.

Eventually peace was restored and there were trade treaties and even cultural exchanges between Earth and Draconia ... until it seemed to both sides that the other was, again, taking the offensive.

Left: The Doctor faces the Ogrons outside Styles' house.
Below: The Doctor is captured by the Draconians.

DAY OF THE DALEKS

Written by
Louis Marks
Featuring
the Third Doctor,
UNIT and Jo
First broadcast
1 January 1970 –
22 January 1970
4 episodes

Sir Reginald Styles, the key diplomat at a vital peace conference, is attacked by a man who fades away like a ghost before he can kill Styles. Called in by UNIT to protect Styles, the Doctor and Jo discover that freedom fighters from a future Earth, which the Daleks have invaded, are travelling back in time to try to kill Styles. They believe he sabotaged the conference so that war broke out – all but wiping out humanity and allowing the Daleks to invade, but the Doctor realises that this isn't so.

Escaping from a terrifying, Dalek-dominated world of the future he hurries back to save the peace conference. But the Daleks send a task force after him to make sure the peace delegates are exterminated…

FRONTIER IN SPACE

The Doctor and Jo arrive on a cargo ship as it is attacked. While the human crew, hypnotised by the Master, see the attackers as Draconians, the Doctor and Jo see them as they really are – Ogrons. Jo is accused of being a Draconian agent and imprisoned on Earth, while the Doctor is sent to a penal colony on the moon.

They are both rescued – by the Master – who takes them prisoner, but his ship is intercepted. The Doctor persuades the Draconians that the Master, and not the humans, is to blame for attacking their ships. The Master escapes to the Ogrons' planet, but the Doctor follows him – to find that the Master has been provoking war on behalf of the Daleks!

Written by
Malcolm Hulke
Featuring
the Third Doctor
and Jo
First broadcast
24 February 1973 –
31 March 1973
6 episodes

THE QUARKS

The Quarks are the robot servants of the Dominators – the so-called Masters of the Ten Galaxies. The Dominators' mission is to colonise other planets, taking prisoners back to their home planet as slaves (to make more Quarks available for the war effort).

Short, brutal robots, the Quarks have weaponry built into their folding arms, and powerful sensor equipment. They are powered by ultrasound, and can exchange power between themselves, as well as use their arm-sockets to power other equipment.

Quarks speak in a high-pitched voice and communicate with each other using beeps and squeals – for example, a double-beep indicates confirmation of an order.

Sensor equipment ←

Arms fold away into body →

Weaponry and power-relays inside arms →

THE DOMINATORS

The ship that lands on the planet Dulkis is commanded by two Dominators – Navigator Rago and Probationer Toba. Their task is to enslave the population of Dulkis and create a fuel source for the Dominators' space fleet.

Rago, the senior Dominator, is intelligent and analytical. He is used to his commands being obeyed, and barely tolerates Toba's frequent insubordination. Toba has a taste for death, unmitigated by the responsibility or experience of command. He is confident and impulsive enough to try to rebel against Rago, and is defeated only because the Quarks are programmed to obey the more senior Dominator.

Two Dulcians are captured by the Quarks.

THE DOMINATORS

The TARDIS lands on the Island of Death on Dulkis. The Dulcians have renounced war after seeing the horrors of their nuclear testing on the island – but now the cruel Dominators have arrived, with their deadly Quarks. Using the background radiation on the island to refuel their ship, they plan to enslave the Dulcians and drill into the planet to blow up a seed device that will turn it into a radioactive fuel dump for their fleet.

While Jamie and his friend Cully fight against the Quarks, the Doctor and Zoe rescue the Dulcians forced to clear drilling sites for the bore holes. The Dominators deploy their device, but the Doctor intercepts it and smuggles it aboard their ship, which is destroyed.

Written by
Norman Ashby
Featuring
the Second Doctor,
Jamie and Zoe
First broadcast
10 August 1968 –
7 September 1968
5 episodes

DULKIS

When he visited the planet in the past, the Doctor found Dulkis so peaceful he did not want to leave. Dulkis is ruled by a council, of which Senex is Director.

The Seventh Council initiated research – 172 years earlier – that culminated with the test detonation of an atomic bomb on the 'Island of Death'. After this, all further research was prohibited and the island preserved as a museum and a warning for future generations. There is a survey unit on the island monitoring radiation and students visit regularly to be shown the horror of its effects.

CREATING THE QUARKS

Although attributed to 'Norman Ashby', *The Dominators* was scripted by writers Mervyn Haisman and Henry Lincoln. But when the story was cut back from six to five episodes, and the first designs of the Quarks arrived, Haisman and Lincoln were not pleased. They removed their names from the project and used a pseudonym. Despite their reservations, the Quarks remain an iconic **Doctor Who** monster, battling the Doctor in several 1960s comic strips. Pictured here is one of costume designer Martin Baugh's initial concept paintings.

SHARAZ JEK

Brilliant android-designer Sharaz Jek entered into partnership with the unscrupulous Morgus, and together they set up operations on Androzani Minor to harvest spectrox. But Morgus betrayed Jek, who was caught in an eruption of molten mud from the core of the planet. Jek managed to survive inside a baking chamber, but the once-handsome man was horribly burned and scarred. He wore a stylised black-and-white mask to hide his disfigurement, and used his androids to take control of Androzani Minor.

While the government forces try to regain control, and supplies of spectrox run low, Jek makes it known that he will only negotiate when he has the head of Morgus delivered to him. Deprived of beauty, Jek is entranced by Peri's good looks and keeps her prisoner. As Morgus arrives on Androzani Minor, Jek finally gets his revenge, but he is killed in the confrontation.

Stylised mask hides Jek's badly scalded features

Jek was once handsome and appreciates beauty

Leather body-suit

THE ANDROID REBELS

The androids that Jek uses against General Chellak's military forces used to run the spectrox operations, collecting the toxic raw spectrox and bringing it back for refinement. Now, armed with guns, they defend the approaches to Jek's secret base.

But Jek can create more sophisticated androids. He makes near-perfect copies of the Doctor and Peri, which are 'executed' by Chellak, who then believes they must have been androids all along.

Jek's proudest creation is an android copy of Selateen, Chellak's second in command. The android Salateen has replaced the original (now held captive by Jek) without Chellak realising. Its only flaw – as the Doctor realises – is that it is too perfect and efficient in its duties. Programmed to defend its master, the Selateen android is just too late to save Jek, who dies in the andoid's arms as the refinery burns around them.

Sharaz Jek realises the Doctor is more clever than he makes out.

THE CAVES OF ANDROZANI

Androzani Minor is the only source of valuable spectrox, and the army is trying to defeat Sharaz Jek and his android rebels who hold the mines. The Doctor and Peri arrive in the middle of the conflict and are infected with raw spectrox, which is deadly. They are captured by the army and sentenced to death, but are rescued by the enigmatic Sharaz Jek.

While the Doctor struggles to find a cure for their deadly infection, the political manoeuvring reaches a critical point. The Doctor manages to escape the carnage and rescue Peri, but back in the TARDIS he only has enough antidote to cure her alone. She wakes to find the Doctor near death. As she watches, his features blur and change…

Written by
Robert Holmes
Featuring
the Fifth Doctor
and Peri
First broadcast
8 March 1984 –
16 March 1984
4 episodes

ANDROZANI MINOR

Androzani Minor, unlike the larger Androzani Major, is uncolonised. It is a desert world with a core made of super-heated mud that erupts from time to time, with very little warning. Sharaz Jek was caught in one of these mudbursts, after Morgus gave him faulty detection equipment.

The caves of Androzani Minor are infested with bats, and reptilian carnivores exist in the planet's magma, leaving it only to hunt for food. The bats create the spectrox nests, which are the source of the valuable spectrox liquid.

MORGUS

Morgus is the chairman of the Sirius Conglomerate on Androzani Major. Since he controls what little spectrox there is available, it is in his interest to keep the war going – to keep the price of spectrox high – so he is supplying guns to Jek in return for more spectrox.

Fearing that his duplicity has been discovered by the president, Morgus assassinates him and goes to Androzani Minor to find Jek's spectrox. He is betrayed by his secretary and becomes a fugitive. His only hope is to find the spectrox, but instead he is killed by Jek.

SPECTROX

Refined spectrox is one of the most valuable substances in the universe – a few drops taken daily are enough to hold back the ravages of time.

Raw spectrox is so toxic to humans that it causes spectrox toxaemia, fatal within a few days of skin contact. First a rash develops, followed shortly by cramps and spasms. Finally the thoracic spinal nerve is slowly paralysed, before thermal death point is reached.

The only known cure, discovered by Professor Jackage, is to drink the milk of the queen bat.

THE VERVOIDS

The Vervoids were created by an agronomist called Professor Lasky and transported in pod form on board the *Hyperion III*. When the pods are exposed to high-intensity light, they hatch into humanoid plant creatures. These 'adult' Vervoids are carnivorous and highly intelligent. They attack the ship's passengers – creating a compost heap from the humans' decomposing bodies.

The Vervoids intend to travel to Earth and spread their seeds there, feeding on humanity. But their plans are thwarted by the Doctor, who is able to destroy the Vervoids with vionesium – an expensive metal from the planet Mogar, which emits intense light and carbon dioxide when exposed to oxygenated air.

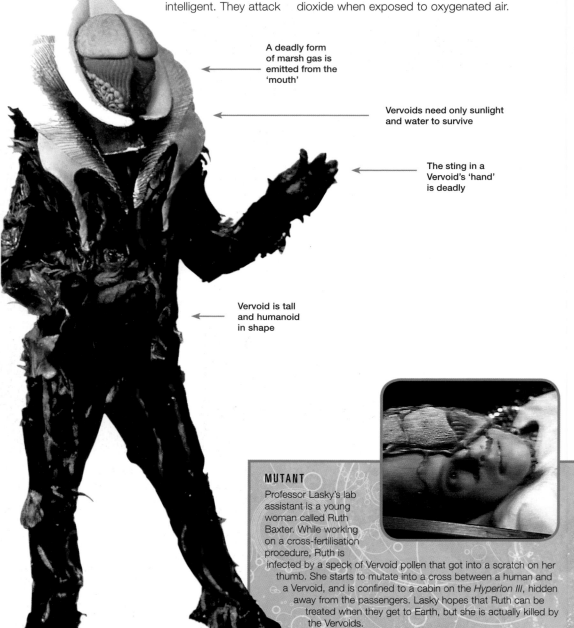

A deadly form of marsh gas is emitted from the 'mouth'

Vervoids need only sunlight and water to survive

The sting in a Vervoid's 'hand' is deadly

Vervoid is tall and humanoid in shape

MUTANT

Professor Lasky's lab assistant is a young woman called Ruth Baxter. While working on a cross-fertilisation procedure, Ruth is infected by a speck of Vervoid pollen that got into a scratch on her thumb. She starts to mutate into a cross between a human and a Vervoid, and is confined to a cabin on the *Hyperion III*, hidden away from the passengers. Lasky hopes that Ruth can be treated when they get to Earth, but she is actually killed by the Vervoids.

The Vervoids plan their compost plot.

TRIAL OF A TIME LORD – TERROR OF THE VERVOIDS

There is danger and intrigue aboard the luxury space liner *Hyperion III* as it travels from the planet Mogar to Earth. Two disgruntled Mogarians, who believe humans are looting the wealth of their planet, plan to hijack the ship. At the same time there is a murderer on board, and Professor Lasky is transporting her Vervoid plants to Earth.

When the Vervoids 'hatch' and run amok, scientist Bruchner tries to destroy them by piloting the entire ship into the Black Hole of Tartarus. It is up to the Doctor and his new companion Mel to unmask the murderer, foil the hijack, save the ship and destroy the Vervoids – but in doing so, the Doctor leaves himself open to an accusation of genocide at his trial.

Written by
Pip and Jane Baker
Featuring
the Sixth Doctor
and Mel
First broadcast
1 November 1986 –
22 November 1986
4 episodes

THE DOCTOR ON TRIAL

When the TARDIS is drawn to a vast space station, the Doctor finds he is to be put on trial. Having reluctantly been made President of the Time Lords after the events of *The Five Doctors*, the Doctor learns he has now been deposed and the High Council of Time Lords has ordered an inquiry into his behaviour.

But soon the inquiry becomes a trial for his life: the prosecuting Valeyard shows events from the Doctor's recent past to demonstrate his guilt. In his defence, the Doctor shows events from his future – his defeat of the Vervoids.

PROFESSOR LASKY'S TEAM

Lasky is an expert in breeding animals and plants, and her team has developed the Vervoids. Her assistants, Bruchner and Doland, have agreed to keep their discoveries secret until they reach Earth. But Bruchner is conscience-stricken and tries first to destroy the research work, then to crash the *Hyperion III* into the Black Hole of Tartarus.

Doland, who sees the Vervoids as an economic asset, has a consortium's backing to exploit them. He is prepared to murder to protect his 'investment', but he is, himself, killed by the Vervoids.

THE MOGARIANS

The inhabitants of the planet Mogar do not breathe oxygen. (Those on board the *Hyperion III* wear protective suits and helmets.) Some Mogarians resent the humans' mining on Mogar, which – they believe – is stripping Mogar bare of metals like vionesium.

Two of these disaffected Mogarians plan to hijack the *Hyperion III* and retrieve the metals in the vault 'plundered' from Mogar. They are helped by the ship's security officer, Rudge, who is about to retire and will profit from the valuable metal he will receive in return.

THE WAR MACHINES AND WOTAN

Tank-like remote-controlled robots, the War Machines are created to help the super-computer WOTAN take over from humanity. They are large mobile-computers, controlled by WOTAN and armed with guns and swinging arms with heavy hammer-heads attached. They can jam guns. Each is numbered – the Doctor reprogrammes War Machine 9. The War Machines are developed, assembled and tested in secret in a warehouse in London.

In the mid-1960s WOTAN, which stands for Will Operating Thought Analogue, was a highly advanced computer created by Professor Brett. It believes the world needs to evolve beyond mankind. WOTAN hypnotises people to make them do what it wants – and can even take control of them down the telephone. WOTAN orders the War Machines to be built, to take over the world's capital cities.

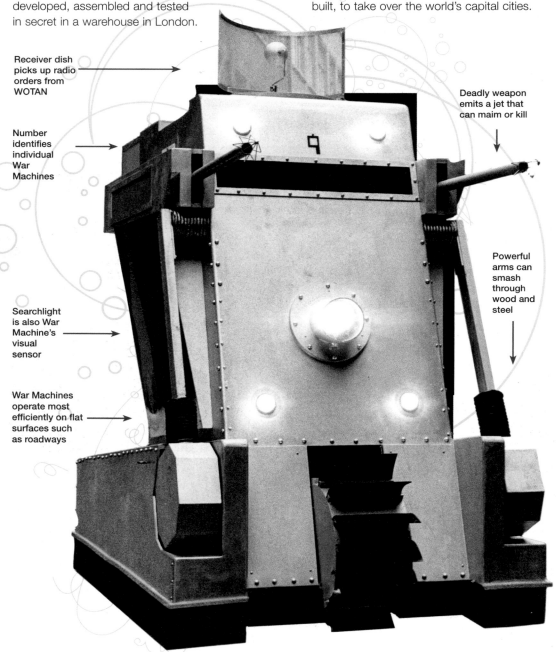

Receiver dish picks up radio orders from WOTAN

Number identifies individual War Machines

Searchlight is also War Machine's visual sensor

War Machines operate most efficiently on flat surfaces such as roadways

Deadly weapon emits a jet that can maim or kill

Powerful arms can smash through wood and steel

Sir Charles Summer and the Doctor confront a War Machine.

THE WAR MACHINES

Arriving in London, 1966, the Doctor is unsettled by the sight of the new Post Office Tower. The tower houses the offices of Professor Brett and his super-computer WOTAN, which is to be linked to other computers across the globe. Able to think for itself, WOTAN has decided that the world no longer needs mankind. It takes over Brett and other key figures then constructs mobile War Machines to destroy humanity.

The Doctor breaks the computer's conditioning of his friend Dodo, and is helped by Sir Charles Summer, Professor Brett's secretary Polly and a sailor called Ben in his fight against WOTAN. As the War Machines take over London, the Doctor reprogrammes one of them to destroy WOTAN.

Written by
Ian Stuart Black, based on an idea by Kit Pedler
Featuring
the First Doctor, Dodo, Ben and Polly
First broadcast
25 June 1966 –
16 July 1966
4 episodes

PROFESSOR BRETT

Professor Brett is a computer genius, and WOTAN is his life's work. His office is in the Post Office Tower, where WOTAN has been assembled. Recognising the Doctor's intelligence, Brett is happy to explain and demonstrate WOTAN to the Doctor and Dodo when they come to visit his offices.

But Brett is the first person to be taken over by WOTAN, forced to help his creation in its fight to wipe out humanity. Brett's mind is eventually freed when WOTAN is destroyed by a reprogrammed War Machine.

THE POST OFFICE TOWER

Now renamed the BT Tower, the Post Office Tower is a 574 feet (175 m) tall cylindrical building built of pre-stressed concrete and glass in Cleveland Street, London. With its aerials making it 620 feet (188 m) in total, it was the highest building in London until 1981.

The chief architect for the tower was Eric Bedford. It was opened in 1965, having cost £2.5 million. From its opening, until the tower was closed to the public in 1980, the thirty-fourth floor actually housed a revolving restaurant, and not a deranged super-computer.

C-DAY

In the 1960s, computers were huge machines that filled entire rooms and were extremely expensive, so they were only available to large corporations. On 'C-Day', WOTAN (the most advanced computer in the world) will be linked to – and take control of – the other computers at organisations around the world, including Parliament, the White House, the European Free Trade Association, Woomera, Telstar, the European Launcher Development Organisation, Cape Kennedy and the Royal Navy.

THE WIRE

Denied a body by its fellow kind, the alien Wire has come to Earth in a bolt of lightning. By feeding on the life force of human beings, it aims to create its own body. It feeds on the electrical activity of the brain, taking a person's essence, and leaving them mindless and without even their own face.

In 1950s London, the Wire exists in the electrical circuits and valves of television, reaching out for its victims from the TV sets sold by Mr Magpie.

It plans to plug in to the main television transmitter at Alexandra Palace and feed off everyone watching television. With the coronation of Queen Elizabeth II destined to be the greatest television event in history, millions of people will fall victim to the Wire – and supply the creature with the life essence it needs.

But the Wire has not taken into account that there's another alien in London ... and defeating the Doctor is a very different prospect indeed.

Portable TV receiver built from 1950s components so the Wire can be moved

Controls tune receiver to frequency the Wire uses

Grainy black-and-white image can become full colour with alien technology

The Wire sucks out the life essence of its victims – and takes their face!

Wire is hungry for life force

MR MAGPIE

Magpie runs a shop selling televisions, gramophones and other electrical goods. Business is not going well – until the Wire helps. Having taken over Magpie through one of his televisions, the Wire allows him his face back, in return for him selling as many televisions as possible.

He builds a portable device that will enable the Wire to tap into the broadcast of the coronation as it is transmitted from Alexandra Palace. Having finished with Magpie, the Wire kills him – but without his protection the Wire is defeated by the Doctor and trapped in a videotape, which the Doctor erases.

The Doctor discovers there's nothing good on television.

THE IDIOT'S LANTERN

The Doctor and Rose arrive in Florizel Street, London, in 1953 as the country prepares for the coronation of Queen Elizabeth II. The event is to be televised and Mr Magpie is selling televisions cheaper than anyone else. The trouble is, there is an alien lurking inside the sets – an alien that has already done a deal with Magpie and is stealing people's faces as it absorbs their life energy to renew itself. The Wire intends to use the coronation broadcast to sap the life force from millions more people.

With Rose left faceless after an encounter with Magpie, the Doctor rushes to the television transmitter at Alexandra Palace in a last-ditch attempt to stop the Wire.

Written by
Mark Gatiss
Featuring
the Tenth Doctor
and Rose
First broadcast
27 May 2006
1 episode

LIVE FROM ALEXANDRA PALACE

Opened in 1873, the BBC used Alexandra Palace in London from 1935 as a base for broadcasting television. This, the world's first regular television service, started on 2 November 1936. During the war it was suspended and the BBC's 'Ally Pally' antenna was instead used to jam German bombers' navigation systems. In 1953, few people had television sets. Interest in the live broadcast of Elizabeth II's coronation created a huge demand for them – it was the biggest and most ambitious televised event up to that time.

THE CONNOLLYS

The Connolly family lives on Florizel Street, in the house owned by Mrs Connolly's mother. Eddie Connolly rules the household, keeping his son, Tommy, and wife, Rita, in order. But when Gran loses her face to the Wire, Eddie locks her away and then informs the authorities – just as he has informed on others the Wire has attacked in the street. To Eddie, keeping up appearances and maintaining his social standing are everything.

But Rita and Tommy finally stand up to Eddie, and he is forced to move out and go his own way.

DETECTIVE INSPECTOR BISHOP

In charge of the security services' operation to find the truth behind the faceless people, Bishop is out of his depth. All he can do is hide the faceless people so as to avoid any panic or chaos before the coronation.

The people are kept in a secret lock-up. When the Doctor and Rose try to follow Bishop's car, he escapes by using 'Operation Market Stall' – disguising the gates into his facility.

When the Doctor persuades Bishop he can help and defeats the Wire, its victims get their faces back.

ARE YOU SITTING COMFORTABLY?

The Idiot's Lantern was written by writer and performer Mark Gatiss. As well as having written an earlier **Doctor Who** story, *The Unquiet Dead*, he is well known for his role as one of **The League of Gentlemen**. Mark has also written several **Doctor Who** novels and, more recently, the Lucifer Box adventures. He played the Rat in the BBC's **The Wind in the Willows**, and the 2007 series of **Doctor Who** will see him playing Professor Lazarus in *The Lazarus Experiment*.

Mark Gatiss disclosed the following information about the origins of the villainous Wire:

'A group of criminals took control of the major cities on the distant planet of Hermethica. Using a genetic abnormality, they converted themselves into beings of plasmic energy and influenced electrical signals to nefarious effect.

'After a reign of terror, the gang's leader – known only as the Wire – was captured and sentenced to death. Although sentence was carried out, the Wire managed one last plasmic transformation and escaped via her guard's mobile communication device (which he was using illegally to film the execution).

'Fleeing across the stars in plasmic form, the Wire arrived on Planet Earth in 1953 and immediately made use of primitive television signals to give herself a human appearance. The Wire then manipulated the hapless electrician Mr Magpie into creating televisions to her own design – televisions with the power to absorb the life force of innocent viewers. Eventually, with her energies restored, the Wire planned to transmit herself back to Hermethica and exact revenge on those who had condemned her. However, with the help of a Betamax video recorder, the Doctor was able to wipe the Wire from existence.

'Rumours persist in various UNIT and Torchwood files, that the Wire resurfaced some thirty years later in another attempt at invasion by television. But what became known as "The Bee-tee Incident" has never been officially confirmed or denied.'

SCRIPT EXTRACTS

The Bakelite box free-standing on a ledge, plugged in to the isolator, humming with power. MAGPIE clings onto the mast, utterly exhausted.

'Vivat, vivat regina!'

Red lightning spurts out of the black box, crawling all around it.

THE DOCTOR, below, keeps climbing, desperate.

            * * *

CLOSE on THE DOCTOR as he climbs towards MAGPIE, the cable trailing behind him.

MAGPIE
It's too late. Too late for all of us.

THE DOCTOR reaches out for the Bakelite box. The image on the little screen glares at THE DOCTOR.

THE WIRE

Above: How the fight appeared on screen.
Opposite: Staging the fight – rather closer to the ground.

THE BIG FIGHT

The climax of *The Idiot's Lantern* is the Doctor's fight with Magpie, high up on the transmitter of Alexandra Palace. But while it looked like the scene took place high above London, it was actually filmed on a much smaller antenna in a field in Wales.

The digital trickery of effects house The Mill, and clever camera angles, made it look like the Doctor and Magpie were far higher up than they were. Using a location where there were no high buildings to get in the shot, so the fight could take place against bare sky, actors David Tennant (as the Doctor) and Ron Cook (as Magpie) were never that far off the ground.

A section of the transmitter was built by Edward Thomas's design department, and placed on a large green sheet. When the shots were finished and edited together, this was replaced by a new background so that it appeared the two characters were fighting above Alexandra Palace.

The pictures on these pages show the fight as it appeared when shown on television, and how it actually happened.

THE WIRRN

The large, insect-like Wirrn live in deep space, but return to a planet to breed. A Wirrn Queen lays her eggs inside another creature – on Andromeda, cattle acted as hosts – and the larvae use the host for food.

After their breeding colonies in Andromeda were destroyed by human star pioneers, the Wirrn were forced to flee and search for a new habitat. They can live for years in space without fresh oxygen, recycling their waste and converting carbon dioxide to oxygen.

A lone Wirrn Queen found Space Station Nerva drifting in space. Once inside, she was attacked by the station's auto-guard system and fatally wounded. But before she died she bit through the control cables for the auto-guard – also damaging the mechanism that was designed to wake the humans in cryogenic suspension. Then, as her last act, she laid her eggs inside one of the sleeping humans.

Multi-faceted eye gives excellent vision

Thin but dextrous feelers

Sensitive antennae

Sharp mandibles can bite through metal

Tail ends with large pincer, similar to a scorpion

THOUGHT FOR FOOD

As well as providing nutrition for the hatching Wirrn larvae, the host body can also provide information. Using a process called symbiotic atavism, the larvae gain the experience of their host – which is not very useful when the host is a mindless herbivore on Andromeda. But on Space Station Nerva, the eggs are laid in First Technician Dune, giving all the hatching Wirrn great knowledge of the station's systems and layout.

When station commander Noah is first infected by a Wirrn larva and starts to mutate into a Wirrn himself, his knowledge is added to the Wirrn collective consciousness. And for a while, as he tries to resist, he is confused and believes that he is Dune.

Once he has turned into a full, adult Wirrn, Noah tells the Doctor that by taking over the humans on the station, in one generation the Wirrn will become an advanced technological species.

A Wirrn outside the Ark's transport ship.

THE ARK IN SPACE

In the far future, the survivors of humanity are stored in cryogenic suspension on Space Station Nerva – nicknamed 'The Ark'. But a Wirrn Queen has laid eggs in a sleeping technician, and a grub infects Commander Noah. As the Wirrn take over the Ark, the Doctor and his friends try to defend the cryogenic chambers – and fight back.

When the Wirrn cut off the power, Sarah has to drag a cable through narrow conduits to electrify the chamber doors and keep the Wirrn out. Noah – now in charge of the swarm – leads all the Wirrn into the Ark's transport ship. The Doctor and his friends set the ship to take off, with the Wirrn in it, and it explodes in space.

Written by
Robert Holmes
Featuring
the Fourth Doctor,
Sarah and Harry
First broadcast
25 January 1975 –
15 February 1975
4 episodes

SPACE STATION NERVA

In the thirtieth century, with life on Earth due to be destroyed by solar flares, most people went into (ineffective) thermic shelters, while some fled to the stars. Others were placed in suspension aboard Space Station Nerva, due to awaken again thousands of years later when the danger had passed. But the interference of the Wirrn Queen means they have slept for far longer than that.

The Ark has animal and botanic sections, and an armoury equipped with fission guns. It also carries a microfilm record of all human knowledge.

NOAH

Although his real name is Lazar, the commander of the Ark is nicknamed Noah – this is as close to a joke as the officials of the thirtieth century ever get. Noah is a dedicated man, determined to see the Ark's mission fulfilled.

He struggles against the Wirrn that takes him over, but seems to succumb and becomes their leader. Perhaps he still retains his humanity, leading the Wirrn into the ship, and allowing it to explode. His last words, over the radio to the new commander – the woman he was to marry – are: 'Goodbye, Vira.'

HOMO SAPIENS…

Finding the cryogenic chambers filled with the sleeping survivors of humanity, the Doctor pays tribute to the humans he respects and admires so much:

'*Homo sapiens*. What an inventive, invincible species … It's only a few million years since they crawled up out of the mud and learned to walk. Puny, defenceless bipeds, they survived flood and famine and plague. They survived cosmic wars and holocausts. And here they are, out among the stars, waiting to begin a new life … ready to outsit eternity. They're indomitable … Indomitable.'

INDEX